A New Look at Black Families

Fifth Edition

Charles Vert Willie and Richard J. Reddick

ALTAMIRA
PRESS

A Division of
ROWMAN & LITTLEFIELD PUBLISHERS, INC.
Walnut Creek • Lanham • New York • Oxford

ALTAMIRA PRESS
A Division of Rowman & Littlefield Publishers, Inc.
1630 North Main Street, #367
Walnut Creek, CA 94596
www.altamirapress.com

Rowman & Littlefield Publishers, Inc.
A Member of the Rowman & Littlefield Publishing Group
4501 Forbes Boulevard, Suite 200
Lanham, Maryland 20706

PO Box 317
Oxford
OX2 9RU, UK

British Library Cataloguing in Publication Information Available

Library of Congress Cataloging-in-Publication Data

Willie, Charles Vert, 1927–
    A new look at Black families / Charles Vert Willie and Richard Reddick.—5th ed.
    p. cm.
    Includes bibliographical reference (p.) and index.
    ISBN 0-7591-0241-4 (hardcover : alk. paper)—ISBN 0-7591-0242-2 (pbk. : alk.
paper)
    1. African American families. I. Reddick, Richard, 1972– II. Title.

E185.86 .W55 2003
306.8'089'96073—dc21   2002012460

Printed in the United States of America

∞™ The paper used in this publication meets the minimum requirements of
American National Standard for Information Sciences—Permanence of Paper
for Printed Library Materials, ANSI/NISO Z39.48-1992.

Contents

2893

111049

Preface

This book offers a more refined answer to the question: What is it like to be black in the United States? The more refined answer we try to give disaggregates the black population into affluent, working-class, and low-income family groups. We, then, proceed to answer this question for blacks, according to their varying socioeconomic status categories. This approach prevents stereotyping a whole group for behavior applicable to only one or two population sectors.

Descriptive information is something of value. We offer such data in ten case studies of black women and black men of achievement and in six case studies of black family life in low-income, working-class, and affluent populations, prepared by students in a course taught at the Harvard Graduate School of Education by Charles Willie on "Adaptation and Learning in Majority and Minority Families." Names of students who prepared the case studies are mentioned in the text. However, pseudonyms are used for family names in case studies; other identifying information (such as place of residence, job titles, etc.) has been changed to protect the anonymity of each household. In all instances, substitutions are equivalent to the real features of a family.

To enhance our understanding of the descriptive features of family life, we analyze the family case studies according to well-documented theoretical and conceptual approaches in sociology, particularly those having to do with socioeconomic status-attainment. However, our study goes beyond theories of social stratification and explores three other important adaptation strategies such as alternative routes to excellence exhibited by individuals affiliated with different kinds of families, power-sharing practices among spouses in households of black people, and the cross-gender effects of fathers and mothers on achievement of their male and female offspring.

Finally, we conclude our analysis by determining whether race continues to be significant in the adaptation of families to society at large. Our data about the closing but continuing gap between black and white people regarding education, employment, and income show a diminishing but continuing racial difference that is significant. We also believe that some of the unique adaptation strategies of black people to the U.S. society are significant because they can benefit other households, including households of brown and white people. Among such strategies, is the equitable distribution of social power increasingly found among male and female spouses in black families.

Because of these findings, this book is of value to policymakers, practitioners, and scholars interested in the interaction of racial, socioeconomic, and gender microsocial units and their relationship to the macrosocial organization of society.

Our study and analysis reject the notion that the way of life of any single racial, socioeconomic, or gender group is the mainstream. We believe that the mainstream consists of several tributaries. This fact means that we cannot fully understand white families without also understanding their relationship to black families and brown families; we cannot fully understand black families without understanding their relationship to white families and brown families; and, of course, we cannot fully understand brown families without understanding their relationship to black families and white families. Each of these groups is a tributary or microsocial unit; added together, they, as a collectivity, become the mainstream.

ACKNOWLEDGMENTS

This book is dedicated to the memory of Louis J. and Carrie Sykes Willie and Theodore L. and Isabell Conklin.

—Charles Vert Willie

This book is dedicated to the memory of Lillian Dawes, Catherine Reddick, Norman Thomas, Kermit Ireland, and Maralyn Heimlich.

—Richard J. Reddick

*   *   *

I would like to acknowledge my deep gratitude to my coauthor, mentor, and friend, Dr. Charles Vert Willie, without whom my work on *A New Look at Black Families*, Fifth Edition, would not have been possible. Throughout the writing of this book, Chuck's support and encouragement helped move this edition from concept to reality. I thank him for his generosity of spirit and direction.

I want to thank my mentors who have so ably guided and inspired me over the years. As an undergraduate, Brenda Burt, Renee Polk, Curtis Polk, Jim Vick, and Ricardo Romo influenced me to maximize my opportunities as a campus leader. Eunice Alexander and Shelia Williams were inspirations to me in the classroom. My experience as a doctoral student has been enhanced by the care and concern expressed to me by Frank Tuitt, George Smith, Heather Harding, Dorinda Carter, and Melissa Chabran and my professors Dean Whitla, Stacy Blake-Beard, and Judy McLaughlin. In my professional life, I am indebted to Preston Allen, Suzanne Fritz, Katie O'Dair, Sean Banks, and Brit Katz, who all inspired and encouraged me to pursue my doctorate. I also would like to thank Marcus Wesson for his inspirational design ideas.

My family has always been the driving force behind my work. My mother Beverly, my father Rick, and my sister Shanmatee have supported my intellectual pursuits. My extended family—the Bryans, Reddicks, Thomases, Irelands, Dudleys, Halls, Harts, McDermoths, Walkers, Chungs, and the Bradfords—hold a special place in my heart, and I thank them for their encouragement. I want to acknowledge my friends who have encouraged Chuck and me in this effort. Your warm wishes and gentle encouragement have made all the difference in the writing of this book.

I have been blessed for the past fourteen years with the company of my wife and best friend, Sherry Ann Reddick, and I thank her for her patience and presence.

* * *

The authors acknowledge with appreciation, Ravi Mehra, Publisher of General Hall who nurtured the first edition of this book into print, and Grace Ebron of AltaMira Press, publishers of this edition.

CREDITS

Chapter 8 was coauthored by Charles Willie and Jolene A. Lane and first appeared in *Phylon*, vol. 49, no. 3–4 (2001), pp. 203–217. We are grateful to *Phylon*, published by Clark Atlanta University, for permission to reprint the complete article and also to Temple University for permission to use extensive quotation from *Hope and Dignity* (1983) by Emily Herrington Wilson and Susan Mullally in chapter 8.

I

CONCEPTUAL APPROACHES TO THE STUDY OF BLACK FAMILIES

1

Introduction

The famous biologist, Julian Huxley, said that ideas are too heavy to carry around in one's mind unless they are rolled on wheels of theory. We propose to present and discuss a theoretical framework that will aid in our understanding of variations in adaptations of black families in the United States.

The miracle of the black family is that it has survived and grown stronger over the years. It had, for one thing, to survive the family breakups resulting from the slave trade. It is interesting, as background for this study of the late twentieth and early twenty-first century, to see what Frederick Douglass, born in slavery in 1817, has to say in his autobiography.

> The reader must not expect me to say much of my family. My first experience of life, as I now remember it, . . . began in the family of my grandmother and grandfather. . . . The practice of separating mothers from their children and hiring them out at distances too great to admit of their meeting, save at long intervals, was a marked feature of the cruelty and barbarity of the slave system. . . . It had not interest in recognizing or preserving any of the ties that bind families together or to their homes. My grandmother's five daughters [one of whom was my mother] were hired out in this way, and my only recollections of my own mother are of a few hasty visits made in the night on foot, after the daily tasks were over, and when she was under the necessity of returning in time to respond to the . . . call to the field in the early morning.
>
> Of my father I know nothing. Slavery had no recognition of fathers. . . .
>
> Old master . . . only allowed the little children to live with grandmother for a limited time; . . . as soon as they were big enough they were promptly taken away. . . .
>
> The time came when I must go. . . . I was seven years old (Douglass 1962: 27–33).

Frederick Douglass was an ingenious man. By the age of twenty-one he had escaped from slavery. In disguise he traveled from Maryland to New York and immediately sent for his fiancée, Anna Murray, who was a free woman. They were married and lived together as husband and wife for forty-four years until Mrs. Douglass died in 1882 (Douglass 1962: 20, 204–205).

Booker T. Washington, born in slavery in 1858 or 1859, presented a similar statement of family separation:

> I was born in a typical log cabin. . . . In this cabin I lived with my mother and brother and sister till after the Civil War, when we were all declared free. Of my ancestry I know almost nothing. . . . I have been unsuccessful in securing any information that would throw any accurate light upon the history of my family beyond my mother. . . . In the days of slavery not very much attention was given to family history and family records—that is, black family records. Of my father I know even less than of my mother, I do not even know his name. . . .
>
> My mother's husband, who was [the] stepfather of my brother John and myself, did not belong to the same owner as did my mother. In fact, he seldom came to our plantation. I remember seeing him there perhaps once a year, that being about Christmas time (Washington 1965: 15–16, 30).

Washington reported that during the war, by running away and following the federal soldiers, his stepfather found his way into the new state of West Virginia. "As soon as freedom was declared, he sent for my mother to come to the Kanawha Valley, in West Virginia. . . . My stepfather had already secured a job at a salt-furnace, and he had also secured a little cabin for us to live in" (Washington 1965: 30–31).

These excerpts from *The Life and Times of Frederick Douglass* and *Up from Slavery* by Booker T. Washington tell us two things: first, there was limited opportunity for experiencing a full family life among black slaves; second, former slaves were nevertheless capable of forming enduring family unions. The first fact is usually remembered; the second fact, frequently forgotten.

For years there has been a great debate over where the story of black families in America should begin—on the shores of the Unites States or in Africa. One of the first to examine this question was the famed scholar W. E. B. DuBois: "there is a distinct nexus between Africa and America which, though broken and perverted, is nevertheless not to be neglected by the careful student" (DuBois 1909: 9, cited in Hill 1999: 47).

Wade Nobles believes there is parallelism between African tribalism and the black family unit in America. Specifically, he refers to "the strong kinship bonds found in black extended families" as "positive functional reflections of the sense of Africanity in black communities" (Noble 1978: 22). Yet there are many other ancient customs of African origin that seem to have no vestiges in contemporary black families in America. Particularly in West Africa, the area from which Kunta Kinte (the ancestor of the late author Alex Haley) came, the Islamic influence was strong. A Council of Elders consisting only of men settled the affairs of the community when there were disputes, including disputes within families. Haley said that in Kunta's village, men could charge that their wives failed to respect them, were unduly lazy, were unwilling to make love when their turn came (some West African men had two, three, or four wives). Unless an accused wife presented a strong counterargument, Haley wrote, the Council of Elders would rule that the aggrieved husband could divorce such a wife. The husband could do this simply by setting any three of his wife's possessions outside her hut and "then uttering toward those possessions, three times, with witnesses present, the words, 'I divorce you!'" (Haley 1976: 114–117). The absence of any custom of supreme male authority in contemporary black families in this society causes us to cast doubt on hypotheses of the African origin of most cultural practices among African Americans.

The history of the black family in the United States should be viewed as a miraculous movement from nothing to something. After slavery, black people continued to experience severe handicaps. The higher rate of family instability among blacks compared with whites is probably more a function of contemporary situations and circumstances than of the historic condition of slavery or the African origin of blacks. For example, an indirect association exists between family income and family instability: as the family income decreases, the proportion of families headed by one parent tends to increase. Inadequate income today, resulting from racial discrimination, is the "fearful price" for being black and is the "incredible mistreatment" that "seriously retards the progress of the group as a whole," a fact missed by political scientist Daniel Patrick Moynihan, who tried to blame the contemporary circumstances of blacks on their group's past experiences of slavery. Contemporary poverty, racial discrimination, and family instability are linked. Poverty, or course, can be eradicated, and so can discrimination. Policymakers interested in further stabilizing the black family could be of much help by working for the elimination of racial discrimination in education, employment, and income.

What has precipitated the need for this theoretical discussion are the contrasting conclusions about black family life offered by some of the best social scientists in the nation. For example, Daniel Patrick Moynihan, who served as a senior staff member of the U.S. Department of Labor during the administration of President Lyndon B. Johnson and later as a senator from New York, reported in 1965 his observation of "deep-seated structural distortions in the life of [African Americans]." He called these "structural distortions" such as broken families, illegitimate births, unemployment, low IQ scores, and receipt of public welfare assistance, a "tangle of pathology." And he said, this pathology "is capable of perpetuating itself" (U.S. Department of Labor 1965: 47). That same year, Robert Coles, a psychiatrist, declared "there's sinew in the black family" (Coles 1965: E1); it has not broken down. From his perspective, the black family has survived and grown stronger. Coles seems to be focusing on resilience in the black family while Moynihan seems to be focusing on pathology. It is of value to understand both forms of adaptation.

Andrew Billingsley, a sociologist, describes African Americans as "a most resilient and adaptive people" (Billingsley 1968: 38). And sociologist Robert Hill has written a book about the strength of families in this population (Hill 1977).

While Billingsley and Hill were trying to understand the uniqueness of black-family resilience, other social scientists such as John Scanzoni were trying to understand how to refashion contemporary black families so that they may fit the pattern of the dominant society (Scanzoni 1971: 4). Scanzoni believed, as did Moynihan, that the family structure of African Americans "seriously retards the progress of the group as a whole" (U.S. Department of Labor 1965: 29), because "it is clearly a disadvantage for a minority group to be operating on one principle, while the great majority of the population and the one with the most advantages . . . , is operating on another" (U.S. Department of Labor 1965: 29). Scanzoni offered a hypothesis similar to the one stated by Moynihan: "there is an association between possession of resources . . . that activists would like to see all blacks have, and the dominant American family pattern" (Scanzoni 1971: 4).

The Moynihan and Scanzoni hypotheses suggest that if black people (the minority) want resources, goods, and services that are similar to those possessed by most white people (the majority), they must fashion their families and other behaviors in the images of those manifested among white people. These hypotheses are at odds with findings by Robert Merton that "it is not infrequently the case that the noncomforming minority in society represents[s] the interests and ultimate values of the group more effectively than the conforming majority" (Merton 1968: 421). The Mertonian observation is not an endorsement of the notion that blacks and their families must learn to act like white people to participate in fulfilling the goals of this society and experiencing its benefits.

Sociologist Bart Landry reports that "the Civil Rights Movement and a booming economy in the 1960s [resulted in] . . . the black middle class doubl[ing] in size" (Landry 1987: 2–3). Landry said these two events "culminat[ed] in equal employment opportunity laws" (Landry 1987: 73). Thus, "the most radical changes in black social structure [resulting in a significant increase in middle-class families] came in the . . . decade . . . [that] combin[ed] prosperity and legal incentives" (Landry 1987: 75).

These events that benefited a microsocial unit of society such as black families were targeted on the macrosocial system, its civil rights laws, and employment practices. Action strategies that focus on individuals or microsocial units only are not likely to have the desired effect. Thus, refashioning black families in the image of white families seems to be an approach that, alone, is probably less effective unless it is combined with a strategy to reconstruct the macrosocial system of institutions and agencies so that resources and opportunities are distributed in ways that are fair and equitable to all individuals and groups. This idea of dealing with both microsocial and macrosocial units of society is consistent with the principle that social structures are effective in maintaining society if they support and sustain its individuals and groups. As stated in *Theories of Human Social Action* (1994), "the macro unit is basic in the social system. This fact means that the microsocial units [such as black families] should never be classified as deviant or outside the mainstream [the macro structure]. They are what they are because of the mainstream" (Willie 1994: 90), and not because of the absence of a macro structure.

Melvin Oliver and Thomas Shapiro address this issue in their book, *Black Wealth/White Wealth, A New Perspective on Racial Inequality* (1995). Their analysis "suggests the need for massive redistributional policies in order to forge the links between achievement, reward, and democracy. These policies must take aim at the gross inequality *generated by those at the very top of the wealth distribution*" (Oliver and Shapiro 1995: 9, emphasis added). Revealed by their study that "blacks and whites . . . face different structures of investment opportunity as well as different financial rewards for performing similar work, Oliver and Shapiro declare that "state policy, [policy of the macro structure] has impaired the ability of many black Americans to accumulate wealth" (Oliver and Shapiro 1995: 4), and has resulted in race differences in wealth holding among families.

Reynolds Farley and Walter Allen conclude that "the best . . . explanations for race differences in the organization of family life in contemporary U.S. society would seem to be those that attribute importance to race differences in functional relationships with the larger society and its institutions" (Farley and Allen 1987: 187). The institutions in society to which they refer have to do with economic well-being, political power, and social standing sometimes called socioeconomic status. "These—more so than differences in values and predispositions—explain the observed differences in family organization and process" (Farley and Allen 1987: 187). Farley and Allen do not rule out cultural uniqueness, including cultural values, as helping to explain race differences in family wealth and family organizations. They declare that these are as valid as institutional actions, but that institutional effects are "the best single category of explanations" for race differences in the organization of family life (Farley and Allen 1987: 171, 187). Based on this analysis, we believe that a study of black families must consider their unique cultural adaptations to society and its institutions as well as the differential adaptations by society and its institutions to various racial and cultural groups.

Thus, it was inappropriate for E. Franklin Frazier to characterize middle-class black families at the midpoint of the twentieth century as living in "a world of make-believe;" which is to say, they were engaged in activity outside the mainstream that emphasized striving for status and prestige, social life through participation in many social clubs, competition for recognition, and conspicuous consumptions such as buying homes, large automobiles, and furniture (Frazier 1957: 195–212). One wonders why Frazier characterized such behavior as make-believe activity for blacks but not for whites.

It would appear that middle-class black families in the 1950s, when Frazier lodged this charge of living in a world of unreality against them, were not very different from middle-class white families at that time described by A. B. Hollingshead (1949). He found that white middle-class families contented themselves with striving for security, owning their well-kept homes, and spending most of their family income on daily living. They also liked to socialize and get together every Saturday night in private homes with cliques of husbands and wives eating, drinking, playing cards, talking, and relaxing in an enjoyable way.

Nevertheless, extreme personal rivalry for coveted offices in community organizations often led to personal feuds among these white middle-class families, since prestige appeared to depend as much on civic leadership as on economic success. There was keen awareness of the way power was exercised among these white families. In addition to deriving prestige from participating in community affairs, a big, new family car and membership in the country club for "golf and gossip" were markers of prestige. And two or three times a year, private parties were given to pay off "social debts" (Hollingshead 1949: 90–95).

It is fair to classify middle-class white families as well as middle-class black families as upwardly mobile strivers who engage in conspicuous consumption, who are desirous of community recognition, and who participate in an active and, sometime frenetic, life of recreational social activity.

Also, it was unfair for William Julius Wilson in 1978 and for Douglas Glasgow in 1980 to declare that low-income black families should be classified as an "underclass" outside the mainstream. If the mainstream is an additive composite of all family units, then low-income families—black, brown, or white—contribute to our common way of life as do working-class families and middle-class families in all racial or cultural groups. We cannot understand one style of family life without examining its relationship to other styles.

Janice Perlman's study of urban poverty and politics in Rio de Janeiro found that a social system may be stable because it is "balanced to the advantage of some [individuals or groups] precisely through the explicit or implicit exploitation of others" (Perlman 1976: 245). Perlman found that the "exploited groups in such a situation are . . . very much integrated into the system, functioning as a vital part of it" (Perlman 1976: 245). Groups classified as being outside the mainstream are very much part of the system; but, according to Perlman, they may be "powerless [people] subject to a good deal of coercion and doing very little coercing" (Perlman 1976: 245).

Low-income families are such people; they may serve as scapegoats for a wide array of societal problems. Perlman found that "they can be considered the source of all forms of deviance, perversity, and criminality and because they lack the means to defend their own actions or image, the self-image of the rest of society can thus be constantly repurified" (Perlman 1976: 259). Perlman found that low-income families "provide much of the vitality for bourgeois culture even while they are disdained by it" (Perlman 1976: 259). Their music, athletic activity, work roles, and worldviews come to mind as illustrations of their way of life that support and sustains interests of the middle class and others in society (Perlman 1976: 259).

Perlman concludes that low-income communities "are playing critical roles in the maintenance of economic, sociocultural, and political system[s]" (Perlman 1976: 261). However, she states, "they can in no sense be regarded as agents of their own destinies" (Perlman 1976: 261). They "can be easily and conveniently manipulated to serve the fluctuating and varying needs of the system" (Perlman 1976: 260).

In the United States, for example, low-income families tended to play, in an obliging way, the roles assigned to them. Frazier said that the spirituals reflected the philosophy of black people, "an attitude of resignation in the face of a hard fate" (Frazier 1957: 118). He said some spirituals focused on life after death and served as "an escape from the evils of the present world" (Frazier 1957: 118). Since the Civil Rights Movement, however, low income black families have become increasingly rebellious; they reject the society that has rejected them, aggressively, and sometimes with criminal behavior (Willie 1985: 12). But low-income white families tend to continue to adapt to society in a stoic, passive, and obliging way, believing that the future will not be different from the past. As stated by one low-income white mother, "I was raised poor; I lived poor and I'm gonna die poor" (Wilkes 1977: 101).

Having recognized different patterns of adaptation to society by different racial or cultural groups among low-income families, we may hypothesize that intergroup differences exist between and within all racial groups in all income levels. This hypothesis is based on data from several sources such as the book *Black and White Families: A Study in Complementarity* (Willie 1985) and another book about *Black Families in White America* (Billingsley 1968). In the latter book, Billingsley reports that "the [African American] experience has not been uniform. It has varied according to time, place and other conditions" (Billingsley 1968: 38). Thus, the theoretical schema we present in the next chapter examines the different worldviews of life, if any, found among black and white people in similar social class levels and the different adaptations, if any, by black and white people in different social class levels.

Social science is indebted to E. Franklin Frazier for his extensive studies on black families (Frazier 1939). A central hypothesis in Frazier's studies during the second trimester of the twentieth century had to do with social stratification: "The social stratification of community . . . would provide the most important frame of reference for studying the social changes in the life of [black] or any other urbanized group" (quoted in Edwards 1968: 141).

Stratification among black families was ignored by many social scientists years ago because of the small number of affluent blacks and also because of the tendency to stereotype all blacks as experiencing a common way of life. By his own reckoning, in a book published near the mid-point of the twentieth century, Frazier said that the black bourgeoisie ranged between one-fifth and one-sixth of all blacks in the Unites States (Frazier 1957: 47).

The final trimester of the twentieth century and the early decades of the twenty-first century present a different set of circumstances. Today (1998 and 1999) approximately one-quarter of black households have an income of fifty thousand dollars and above (U.S. Census Bureau 2000: 466); 45 percent of young black people (sixteen to twenty-four years of age) are enrolled in college (U.S. Census Bureau 2000: 407); and about one-quarter of blacks in the labor force (sixteen years of age and older) are employed in managerial and professional, technical, sales, and administrative jobs (U.S. Census Bureau 2000: 416–417). Based on these data, one may estimate the affluent component of the black population as approximately 25 percent of all black households in the United States today. Therefore, it is inappropriate to say, "A black family is a black family is a black family." Differentiation among blacks is a fact of life.

In this study, we classify black families as low-income or poor if household income is below the official poverty line and if adults in these families have less than a high school education and are employed as laborers or in service occupations, such as private household cleaning, food preparation, or maid and janitorial work. We classify black families as working class if household income is above the official poverty line but at or below the national median income and if adults in the family have not more than a high school education and are employed in precision production and craftwork, such as construction trades, mechanical and repair activities, or personal services occupations. We classify a black family as affluent if household income is above the national median, the adults in the family have attended or graduated from college, and if they are employed in administrative and managerial work, technical specialties, or sales and clerical work. When the adults in a family manifest two out of any three of the characteristics connected with a particular social class position, the entire household is so classified in that position.

One may note that the affluent category in this study does not represent the very wealthy. In 1998 dollars, only 9 percent of black families in the United States had annual incomes that exceeded $75,000. And in 1999, only 11 percent of the adults in black families were employed in managerial and professional specialties. While these proportions represent significant increases, this kind of progress is limited to only one out of every ten black households. For this reason, black millionaires, and especially those who have inherited their wealth from past generations, are not examined in this study.

An important goal of this study is to understand the way of life of black families as microsocial units of this society and to determine how they interact with the macrosocial system. Frazier concluded that blacks had assimilated into the cultural ways of the United States. This belief places him squarely in the social theory camp of structural functionalism. According to Walter L. Wallace, such theorists "define the social in terms of objective behavior relations and seek to explain it by referring to phenomena that are socially generated through characteristics of the participants' environments" (Wallace 1969: 161). Thus, the way of life of black families and differentiation in lifestyles among these families can be understood best by examining their microsocial adaptations and the macroenvironmental settings within which they live.

We continue to analyze Frazier's interest in stratification by understanding how the social system contributes to the adaptation of individuals, groups, and racial populations in the United States. This is an interest that sociologist Robert Merton embraced also. In an essay entitled "Social Structure and Anomie," he designed a systematic approach to the analysis of social and cultural sources of deviant and conformist behavior. Specifically, he wanted to understand "how some social structures exert a definite pressure upon certain persons [and groups] in the society to engage in nonconformist rather than conformist conduct" (Merton 1949: 126). His hypothesis was that groups peculiarly subject to such pressures may manifest fairly high rates of deviant behavior "because they are responding normally to the social situation in which they find themselves" (Merton 1949: 126). If Merton's hypothesis is confirmed, "some forms of deviant behavior, and the equation of deviation and abnormality will be put in question" (Merton 1949: 126).

If Merton's hypothesis is confirmed, it will call to question Frazier's conclusion that blacks, and especially affluent blacks, are outsiders in American life. If Merton's hypothesis is confirmed, it will call to question William

Julius Wilson's conclusion that black ghetto communities are disconnected with the mainstream of United States culture (Wilson 1987: 14). If Merton's hypothesis is confirmed, it will give credence to the notion that the so-called mainstream in social life is a macrosocial concept contributed to by all groups in the social system, including "the underclass" or poor, the working class, and the middle class or affluent. These groups, collectively, may be described as microsocial units, none of which alone should be characterized as the mainstream because affluent people are neither more nor less representative of the total social system than the working class or the poor. If Merton's hypothesis is confirmed, each group will be recognized as responding to the opportunity and liability pressures of the macrosocial system of which it is a microsocial part.

Merton identified three cultural axioms about success in the United States: 1) all should strive for the same lofty goals since these supposedly are open to all; 2) present seeming failure is but a way station to ultimate success; and 3) genuine failure consists only in the lessening or withdrawal of ambition (Merton 1949: 32). These axioms indicate that "American culture continues to be characterized by a heavy emphasis on wealth as a basic symbol of success, without a corresponding emphasis upon the legitimate avenues on which to march toward this goal" (Merton 1949: 33). To Merton, "These axioms represent . . . the deflection of criticism of the social structure onto one's self [or group] among those so situated in the society that they do not have full and equal access to opportunity" (Merton 1949: 133).

Merton believes that some goals in society transcend class lines (Merton 1949: 137, 133). In view of the extended interaction between black and white populations for several centuries in the United States, and also the close association between black families of different social classes in black ghettos of the United States, some goals in common must have developed. For this reason the means-ends schema developed by Merton in his essay "Social Structure and Anomie" appears to be an appropriate theoretical vehicle for explaining adaptations of families by race and social class.

In table 1, (+) signifies "acceptance," (−) signifies "rejection," and (±) signifies "rejection of prevailing values and substitution of new values."

Table 1.1.   A Typology of Modes of Group Adaptation (From Merton 1949: 133)

Modes of Adaptation	Cultural Goals	Institutionalized Means
I. Conformity	+	+
II. Innovation (a)	+	−
III. [Innovation] (b)*	−	+
IV. Retreatism	−	−
V. Rebellion	±	±

*Identified as Ritualism in the original tables by Merton. Type II and III Innovations are similar, with the exception that Type II rejects institutional means and Type III rejects cultural goals.

Merton identifies five kinds of adaptations by individuals to social organization: conformity, innovation, ritualism, retreatism, and rebellion. This typology is a conceptual approach to an understanding of the differences in adaptations among affluent, working-class, and poor families. In this presentation of Merton's schema, Type III, ritualism, has been relabeled as another form of innovation.

Merton recognized the value of situational analysis by calling our attention to the fact "that people may shift from one alternative [adaptation] to another as they engage in different spheres of social activities" (Merton 1949: 133). Thus, he said the categories in the typology "refer to role behavior in specific types of situations, not to personality" (Merton 1949: 133). Adaptations by race and social class then are situationally, not biologically, determined. The situation of blacks in American society, for example, is that of a minority or subdominant population in the power structure that receives an inequitable low amount of the nation's wealth. Thus, the behavior requirements of different groups depend on their situation in the social system, their goals, and the methods available to them for attaining their goals.

Merton states that stability results from adaptation Type I—conformity to both cultural goals and institutionalized means (Merton 1949: 134). This is precisely the adaptation that is manifested by affluent blacks. Far from being isolated from American cultural values, as Frazier claimed, affluent blacks are centrally located in the maintenance of such values. Former U.S. Transportation Secretary, William Coleman, an African American lawyer, once said that whites owe a debt of gratitude to blacks for making the U.S. Constitution work (Willie 1978). It is interesting to note that the most famous black lawyers during two-thirds or more of the twentieth century were constitutional experts. Richard Kluger said that Thurgood Marshall's "record of success as a civil rights lawyer had begun to turn him into a legend" (Kluger 1975: 18).

An analysis of the behavior of affluent black families analyzed in earlier editions of this book revealed them to be conformists to both the cultural goals of success in this nation and the prescribed means for fulfilling these goals. Their values reflected the philosophy of Thomas Jefferson, one of the founders of this nation, who believed that education should be available to all so that the citizens in a democracy could make moral decisions about governance for the common good. Affluent blacks also believe that the institutions of society should protect the weak from the strong and that democratic decision making by the people is a wise way of arriving at just solutions. The values of affluent black families reflect the U.S. Constitution, the legal norm of our society, and its requirement of equal protection of the laws for all.

Black working-class families are Merton's Type IIa adaptation. The black working class is innovative because its members accept the cultural goals of success in our society but reject the means for their achievement, largely because these means are unavailable to them. For the black working class, the opportunity system is partially blocked. Its members experience a closed, not an open, society and must improvise to make their way through. Their adaptation as innovators is according to Type IIa because the working class among blacks strives to overcome and achieve by any means.

The poor are as much a part of society as the members of families in any other social class position. The mainstream values of American culture are well understood by them. Bettylou Valentine (1978: 103) said that these values receive general allegiance among poor blacks. They tend to live in urban ghettos mentioned in earlier editions of this book. Poor blacks appear to have a community support system of kin and friends. Poor blacks are resentful and rage at a discriminating society that they believe has treated them unfairly. As at least one-quarter of the population of African Americans, poor blacks are a sufficient critical mass to demand consideration of their concerns in any social action agenda. Poor black families are rebellious; their adaptation is Merton's Type V. They press for modification in the social structure that will accommodate their concerns and grant them some measure of consideration. They want a society in which there is a "closer correspondence between . . . effort and reward" (Merton 1949: 145). Seeing that the existing society is organized against them, poor blacks veto "business as usual." They do not accept their position as a condition of fate. When they no longer can endure, they riot and rebel, hoping to draw attention to their circumstances, hoping that others will then set things right. Through their rebellion, poor blacks attempt "to change the existing cultural and social structure rather than to accommodate efforts with the structure" (Merton 1949: 379). Merton reminds us, however, that the renegade who "renounces the prevailing values . . . becomes the target of greatest hostility" (Merton 1949: 146). This has been the lot of poor black families. Society has resented and raged against them as much as they have resented and raged against society (Giesen 1973; Jeffers 1970; Schultz 1970).

While the main focus of this book is on the adaptations of black families, material about affluent, working-class, and poor white families will be introduced from time to time to facilitate a brief comparative analysis. Data about white families, used to describe their way of life, were taken largely from case studies collected by Charles V. Willie and published in *Black and White Families* (1985).

Affluent white families subscribe to democracy as a method of social organization but not fully to its goals for success. Their ways of adapting, according to Merton's Type IIIb (as seen in table 2), are those of innovationists in that they seek to change the goals as a way of frustrating those who might lay claim to their privileged position, but they insist that all people use the same agreed-upon means to achieve power and authority in society, although such means may not be available to or suitable for subdominant people in the power structure who do not have a head start. Because affluent white families are anxious

Table 1.2. A Typology of Modes of Adaptation in American Society by Race and Social Class

Social Class	Black Families Mode of Adaptation		White Families Mode of Adaptation	
	Cultural Goals	Institutional Means	Cultural Goals	Institutional Means
Affluent	+	+	−	+
Working Class	+	−	+	+
Poor	±	±	=	=

Note:
+ Conformity to goals or means
− Nonconformity to goals or means
± Resistance to goals or means in an aggressive, rebellious way
= Resistance to goals or means in a passive, retreating way

about whether others may invade their territory or turf, they (in colloquial terminology) try to change the name of the game as a way of eliminating challengers, and they contend that such is fair in a free and open society.

The controversy over school integration is a good example of how affluent whites abide by the procedures of the law but attempt to change the law when it is against them. The plaintiff class, usually blacks and other people of color, filed court cases seeking school integration as a just way of enhancing their education. Somewhere along the way, after plaintiffs won in the court cases, the goal was changed by whites from integration to desegregation. And while there was plenty of evidence that people of color were disproportionately assigned to segregated and less effective schools, the law was changed again so that blacks and other people of color could get relief from having to attend segregated schools only if they could prove that white and black schools were deliberately segregated. Thus, affluent white people did not ignore the law in this nation of laws, but they found ways of changing the law when it did not favor them.

White working-class families appear to be content to settle for a modest place in life. Both mothers and fathers tend to work, usually in clerical or semi-skilled jobs or in service work. The father or husband in the household sometimes looks upon himself as a failure, although he may be a steady worker. Thus the parents tend to invest their dreams in their children's future. This is especially true of the mother or grandmother in the household, who is a chief source of emotional support for the children as well as their mates.

Working-class whites do not blame others for their fate. They tend to see themselves as inadequate for the requirements and responsibilities of their time. For this reason they tend not to have a dream of the kind of life they wish for themselves. They more or less drift, enjoying themselves when possible, conforming to the requirements of the situation in which they find themselves, doing what comes naturally, taking little initiative to change things. White working-class members, therefore, may be classified as conformists, or Type I (as seen in tables 1 and 2). The working-class white family is conformist and adapts according to Type 1—upholding cultural goals and following institutionalized means, believing in self-reliance, accepting the free enterprise system and its opportunities for success or failure. For their circumstances, they blame themselves and not the system. They pledge allegiance to the goals and methods of American society, although the system seems to have left them behind (Wrobel 1976).

In general, poor whites adapt in a retreating fashion, according to Merton's Type IV. They tend to give up on any hope of ever fulfilling culturally prescribed goals for success through legitimate institutional means. One might call such families the socially disinherited who have assimilated the goals, rules, and regulations of society but who have found all avenues to them inaccessible. Merton describes their mode of adaptation as that of frustrated and handicapped individuals who cannot cope and who, therefore, drop out. They experience defeatism and resignation, manifested in escape behavior such as drinking, gambling, and fighting. It is important to recognize that retreatism is a way of reducing conflict that arises from internalization of the legitimate goals and means for achievement and the inability to use the illegitimate route because of internalized prohibitions (Merton 1949: 142–143).

There are few structural supports for poor white families who tend to be isolated from others in rural areas or living as invisible residents of the inner city. They are members of few organizations. Family members work when work is available; but the kinds of jobs that they can hold are neither plentiful nor stable. Thus the women in the household in service occupations are sometimes more regularly employed than their menfolk. The families tend to be stoic and take whatever comes in stride. They do not like to receive charity and boast of the fact that they are not on welfare.

What Robert K. Merton observed in 1949, Peter M. Blau observed in 1987: "macrosociology analyzes the structure of different positions in a population and their constraints on social relations" (Blau 1987: 71). Further, Blau states that the social environment limits our options (Blau 1987: 79). Merton has painted (so to speak) on a large canvas with broad strokes the tendencies of black and white families in different social class positions. However, the processes producing these tendencies are not explained, as Peter Blau reminds us (Blau 1987: 83). Thus we shall consult the literature of our contemporary times to determine if it reinforces what Merton has suggested. We, then, will proceed with an analysis of two case studies of black affluent, working-class, and poor families to further explain why these families adapt to society and their circumstances as they do.

From our initial macrosocial analysis, it is clear that black and white families adapt to a common society in different ways. Our hypothesis is that their different ways of adapting are not only because of their dominant and sub-dominant status in the United States but also because they have symbiotic relationships, as noted by Perlman. Thus we shall invoke the theory of com-plementarity to help us understand why the different racial and socio-economic groups behave as they do.

To sum up this discussion, we declare that it is inappropriate to categorize any group as deviant and, therefore, out of the mainstream. Either deviancy or conformity may be effective responses to the situation in which a group finds itself, and either may be harmful or helpful depending on the situations of group members.

While our concern in this book is largely with understanding the various forms of adaptation found among black families in the United States, we alert the reader to the fact that all groups in society complement each other; no group is self-sufficient. This statement is applicable to the affluent, working class, and poor and to black as well as brown and white people.

Based on our discussion in this introductory chapter, we offer the follow-ing hypotheses that will guide and give direction to our analysis:

1. Black, brown, and white families in the United States share a common core of values that constitutes the macrosocial structure of this national community.
2. Black, brown, and white families adapt to society and its value system in different ways, in part because of the social class positions that mem-bers of each group experience.
3. Black, brown, and white families within the same social class adapt to the society and its social organization differently because of their dom-inant or subdominant status due to the distribution of power resources.
4. The unique adaptations of some racial groups tend to complement the different adaptations that other racial groups have made to the social system and to one another by way of a symbiotic relationship.

All of this is to say that the way of life of one racial group or of one social class cannot be understood apart from the adaptations of the others. Refer-ring to the interdependence of individuals, races, and social class, we are re-minded of the wisdom of George Bernard Shaw's character, Eliza Doolittle, who said that she discovered the difference between a flower girl and a lady is not so much how she acts but how she is treated. Our modified version of her statement is that the difference between individuals, races, and social classes in society is how they act as well as how they are treated.

We hope the theoretical perspective given in this introduction will assist the reader in understanding the case studies and their analysis that follow. Beyond the case studies of black families, we will add analytical chapters on other con-temporary and emerging issues pertaining to the family life of black people.

2

Family Life and Social Stratification

In the tradition of E. Franklin Frazier, we begin our review of the professional literature on studies of black families by examining recent historical trends in lifestyle variations by socioeconomic status. Comparisons are made between black families of different socioeconomic status levels.

The terms *social class, social status,* and *socioeconomic status* are used interchangeably in this study. This is done largely because the investigation is concerned with analyzing lifestyles associated with structural locations in society. Social class, socioeconomic status, or social status are structural variables all having to do with vertical differentiation and hierarchy in social organizations.

Richard Coleman and Lee Rainwater found that "most [people] who prefer upward mobility rest . . . their case for higher rank solely on advances in income and standard of living" (Coleman and Rainwater 1978: 23d). The capacity for black families to satisfy consumption needs is more or less controlled by their disposable income and other sources of wealth available for market transactions. Few blacks today in the United States have access to wealth accumulated by past generations for family members. They, therefore, live largely on wages obtained from current employment in the labor force. Thus, in this study, socioeconomic status is based on occupation, education, and income of household adults.

Community studies by Coleman and Rainwater uncovered a belief system that they attribute to most people in the United States: "First, get an education—that will get you a better job and that will lead to higher social standing, because you will be making more money" (Coleman and Rainwater 1978: 239). W. Lord Warner's index of status characteristics consisted of four variable—occupation, source of income, house type, and dwelling

19

area. In his index, occupation was assigned the highest weight; income was second to it (Warner 1949: 40). A. B. Hollingshead used three factors in his index of social position—ecological area of residence, occupation, and education. He also gave occupation the highest weight and education was second to it (Hollingshead 1949: 27–28). The U.S. Office of Management and Budget offers this summary: "Sufficient education to take part in society and make the most of one's ability, the opportunity to work at a job that is satisfying and rewarding, [and] income sufficient to cover the necessities of life with opportunity for improving one's income" are widely held basic social objectives of this society (U.S. Office of Management and Budget 1973: xiii).

Otis Dudley Duncan reported that average education and average income correlated highly with the prestige scores of occupations; they account for as much as four-fifths of the variance in these prestige scores (Duncan 1961). Early on, in the first trimester of the twentieth century, Robert and Helen Merrel Lynd discovered in their study of Middletown that "money . . . drastically condition[s] the . . . activities of people" in the United States (Lynd and Merrell 1929: 21). And a study in social ecology of residential neighborhoods and areas in Syracuse, New York, revealed that income correlated highly with a five-factor socioeconomic status index including occupation, education, housing condition, and rental or market value. This study revealed that annual family income accounted for about three-fourths of the variance in the status characteristics of neighborhoods (Willie and Wagenfeld 1962: 4).

A definition of poverty by the federal government is used as a guideline in selecting families to represent low-income, working-class, and middle-class households analyzed in this study. The poverty index is based solely on money income and reflects the different consumption requirements of families based on their size and composition. Poverty thresholds are updated ever year to reflect changes in the Consumer Price Index (U.S. Census Bureau 2000: 450).

In 1998, near the beginning of the twenty-first century, about 12 to 13 percent of all people in the United States were classified as impoverished. This proportion varied substantially by race. Only about 10 percent of white people were poor according to federal government guidelines and standards; however, slightly more than one-quarter (26.1 percent) of black people were so classified by the Census Bureau. This proportion of poor blacks represented a reduction from about one-third (33.5 percent) nearly a generation ago to about one-fourth today. However, the proportion of poor people among whites has remained more or less constant over the years—nearly 10 percent since the 1970s (U.S. Census Bureau 2000: 475).

As stated above, case histories of poor black families in this study were selected from those with incomes below the poverty line. Working-class families had incomes above the poverty line at or below the median family income for households in this nation which was $46,737 in 1998 (U.S. Census Bureau 2000: 471). Black families with incomes above the national median were classified as middle class or affluent. In 1998 about 28 percent of all black families (nearly one out of every three) could be classified as middle class or affluent because they had annual family income of fifty thousand dollars or more (U.S. Census Bureau 2000: 471).

For the occupational parameter, divisions by socioeconomic status include three levels: 1) Laborers, unskilled service worker, semiskilled operators, and unemployed adults who have pursued these occupations; 2) people with trades or crafts, technicians, retail sales clerks, and other clerical workers, mechanics, practical nurses, other human service aides, assistants and support staff; and 3) professionals, managers, administrators, accountants, computer programmers, and sales representatives make up the third category of workers. About one-third of the black labor force in 1999 pursued work in the first and lowest category, about one-quarter in the third and highest category, and about two-fifths in the middle-range occupations (U.S. Census Bureau 2000: 416–418).

Education also is divided into three categories for use in this study. The lowest category consists of families whose adult members are without a high school diploma or its equivalent; the second category consists of families whose adult members are high school graduates but have not received a college degree; and the third category consists of families whose adult members are college graduates. In 1999, only about one out of every ten adults in the civilian labor force had less than a high school education; about six out of every ten adults were high school graduates without a college degree; and about three out of every ten adults were college graduates (U.S. Census Bureau 2000: 405). Using this three-tiered educational classification for black adults, 19.5 percent in the civilian labor force in 1999 were college graduates; 67.6 percent were high school graduates without a college degree; and 13 percent were without a high school diploma (U.S. Census Bureau 2000: 405).

Income, an outcome variable, was given greater weight in determining the status position of families in this study. A family with an income in the highest level of this parameter was classified as middle class if any parent in the household also placed in the highest level of the occupational or the educational parameter. Thus, a family was classified as middle class if the family's adult breadwinner was in the two highest levels of the three parameters, provided that one of the two high status levels was income. The same practice was followed in classifying working-class families. A family with an income in the middle level of the three-tier income hierarchy was classified as working class if one or both parents had jobs or education in the middle levels of these two parameters. Finally, poor families were those with income below the poverty line and in which one or both parents had jobs of limited occupational prestige or had received less than a high school education.

This study of black families in three socioeconomic status levels should help us understand what is unique about black families in each status position and what is similar among black families, despite their different status levels. This study, therefore, will examine black families as microsocial units and the black family as a macrosocial unit.

AFFLUENT CONFORMISTS

More than a quarter of a century ago, Willie published an article in the *Journal of Orthopsychiatry* (January 1974) entitled "The Black Family and Social Class" in which he summarized from a socioeconomic perspective the way of life of middle-class, working-class, and low-income African Americans. Descriptions in the remainder of this chapter are based, in part, on findings presented in that article.

Based on the theoretical analysis using the Mertonian schema mentioned in chapter 1, we described middle-class black people as "affluent conformists." We are quick to point out that the conformity characterization is not intended as a negative attribution. Probably the best example of a positive orientation toward conformity by middle-class black people is found in the words and works of Martin Luther King, Jr., one of the esteemed leaders of the Civil Rights Movement in the United States. King, of course, was born into a middle-class, professional family with college-educated parents.

King believed in the law and frequently quoted passages from the Declaration of Independence, the preamble to the Constitution, and the Constitution of the United States. In his first book, he wrote, "the law itself is a form of education. The words of the Supreme Court, of Congress and of the Constitution are eloquent instructors" (King 1958: 175). He offered as illustrations federal court decrees which have "altered transportation patterns, teachers' salaries, the use of recreational facilities" (King 1958: 176). He called segregation and discrimination "strange paradoxes in a nation founded on the principle that all men are created equal" (King 1958: 168). King declared that segregation is basically evil, "because it does not conform with the Declaration of Independence, the Constitution and Supreme Court decision like *Brown v. Board of Education* that outlawed segregation in the public schools" (King 1958: 168).

In family life as well as in political life, middle-class, black people tend to conform to the normative values of the nation. The following trends were noted in Willie's 1974 article.

> Children in black middle-class families tend to be small in number, ranging from one to three, but more often two or less. Continuity in employment is a characteristic of middle class black men.

Public sector jobs . . . have been a source of support and security over the years . . . some black men have . . . received financially rewarding professional positions in industry.

Income is lavishly spent on a home and on the education of children. Middle-class black families tend to trade in older homes for new structures as their income and savings increase. These houses have up-to-date furnishings and modern appliances. For most middle-class black families, their home is their castle and it is outfitted as such.

In most middle-class black families, one member almost always has attended college. Often, both spouses have attended college. Middle class status is directly correlated with increased education. . . .

Children in [black] middle-class households are given music lessons. Daughters, in particular, are expected to learn to play a musical instrument, usually the piano.

Middle class black families in America, probably more so than any other population group in this society, manifest the Puritan orientation toward work and success. For them, work is a consuming experience and little time is available for leisure. Education, hard work, and thrift are accepted as the means for the achievement of success.

To summarize, middle-class black families subscribe to the basic values and goals of American society and utilize appropriately prescribed means for their achievement. Members are success oriented and upwardly mobile.

Property, especially residential property, is a major symbol of success. Conformance with macrosocial values and customs in the United States is best illustrated by middle class black families. (Willie 1974: 52–54)

By 1987, Bart Landry, who has dedicated much of his career in sociology to the study of black middle-class families, reported that "Every attempt was made [by black middle-class families] to become home owners" and that "the home grew in importance . . . as a conformable, secure place . . . furnished as lavishly as possible" (Landry 1987: 59). Landry also discovered serious concern among black, middle-class people about perfecting their occupational skills: "Doctors, lawyers, dentists, school teachers, and other professionals started . . . local and national professional organizations to promote the development of their respective members" (Landry 1987: 63).

Landry declared that "black colleges and universities provided opportunity for the sons and daughters of sharecroppers, laborers, Pullman, porters, domestics, and factory workers to participate in the phenomenon of upward mobility" (Landry 1987: 64). With increasing education and better occupations, Landry said that "middle-class blacks . . . provided the leadership needed by the community[;] . . . some members . . . were elected to public office from black districts and were able to represent the interest of blacks in a formal capacity" (Landry 1987: 65).

The evolution of the black middle class has been a steady incremental growth with the present departing little from the past except in the area of political activity, which has substantially increased in recent years. Much of this has happened because of the Civil Rights Movement that resulted in the Civil Rights Act of 1964 and the Voting Rights Act of 1965. Today, according to Landry, an increasing proportion of black, middle-class families have inherited their middle-class status from their middle-class parents (Landry 2000). This is a recent phenomenon without historical roots. Because the middle class among blacks today recruits from the working class and also reproduces itself, the size of the black middle class now is one-fourth to one-third of all black households.

Landry sees the contemporary black middle class as providing leadership for a new family paradigm called the "egalitarian arrangement" discussed in chapter 9 (Landry 2000: 82). This arrangement has resulted from the dual employment of husband and wife in black families that began several decades ago. Landry said, "these [black] women were far ahead of their time, foreshadowing societal changes that would not occur within the white community for several generations" (Landry 2000: 79). By 1990, nearly seven out of every ten female spouses in black, middle-class families were in the labor force, a number substantially larger than the proportion (slightly above 50 percent) among white female spouses in middle-class families (Landry 2001: 139). By 1990, "31 percent of black . . . middle-class wives had higher incomes than their husbands" (Landry 2000: 144). This is a significant finding, despite the fact that most wives in black middle-class families have incomes that are less than the earnings of the male spouse. Even though fewer wives in black middle-class families earned more than their husbands, earnings of wives are now approximately four-fifths of their husbands' income (Landry 2000: 151). With black, middle-class female earnings tending toward parity with black middle-class men, the egalitarian arrangement in the black community seems to be moving along with a quickening pace. We will discuss this matter and its power implications in greater detail in chapter 9.

The egalitarian arrangement in family structure and function found among blacks, particularly in the middle class, is interesting because it tends to deviate from rather than conform to the prevailing practice of male dominance in white households observed by Daniel Patrick Moynihan in 1965. He said, "Ours is a society which presumes male leadership in private and public affairs. The arrangements of society facilitate such leadership and reward it. A subculture, such as that of the [African] American in which this is not the pattern, is placed at a distinct disadvantage" (U.S. Department of Labor 1965: 29). Not only have black middle-class families rejected Moynihan's prescription of the patriarchal family form, white families are increasingly fashioning their families in the egalitarian model first developed by middle-class black families.

Returning to the matter of conformity, we mention one other activity, that of joining and participating in the affairs of voluntary association. In a recent issue of the *American Sociological Review*, Evan Schofer and Marion Fourcade-Gourinchas assembled useful data on voluntary association membership (Schofer and Fourcade-Gourinchas 2001: 806–828). They state that about 70 percent of the individuals in the United States claim membership in at least one voluntary association and that "People in the United States . . . tend on average to join a greater number of associations" (Schofer and Fourcade-Gourinchas 2001: 807).

In Willie's 1985 study of black, middle-class families, "slightly more than half of the parents [in that study, were] active in church" (Willie 1985: 75). Also, he found that "middle-class blacks are supported through a national network of social clubs, fraternities, sororities, and lodges. These organizations have local chapters that sponsor local events that bring together periodically the black community within a metropolitan area. Moreover, these organizations have annual national gatherings that bring together blacks dispersed throughout the country" (Willie 1985: 75). In this respect, the services rendered by middle-class blacks, especially by way of participating in voluntary association, is in conformity with the national pattern found among whites.

WORKING-CLASS INNOVATORS

Willie described working-class black families as "innovative marginals" (Willie 1974: 238–240) who are betwixt and between the poor and affluent. It is important to clarify that the use of the word *marginal* refers to the fact that many working-class individuals have been or will be exposed to multiple socioeconomic status positions as families in transition. A black working-class family may be a low-income family on its way up or a middle-income household on its way down. Thus, we are not using this term in a pejorative manner. Indeed, individuals as well as groups with multiple socioeconomic or ethnic heritages may have a clearer vision of how to solve macrosocial problems and transcend difficulties. As we have found it helpful elsewhere in this book to use examples from the lives of families that fit the outcome shown in socioeconomic analyses in chapters 6, 7, and 8, we look to the life story of John H. Johnson, founder, chairman, and chief executive officer of the Johnson Publishing Company that owns *Ebony* and *Jet* magazines.

Johnson's acumen as a businessman is legendary, from his initial foray into the print world in 1942 with *Negro Digest* to today, where products such as *Ebony*, *Jet*, *Ebony Male*, and Fashion Fair Cosmetics are household names. Johnson described his family life as a young boy in Arkansas as modest, but not destitute: "We didn't have money, but we weren't—crucial distinction— poor. Our poverty, in other words, couldn't be compared with the soul-crushing poverty in the slums of modern American" (Johnson 1992: 41).

Nevertheless, Johnson's family of orientation was definitely working class. Johnson's mother worked as a domestic servant from time to time; she also washed and ironed clothes. His biological father, who died prematurely, was a laborer and so was his stepfather, who also worked as a deliveryman for a grocery store. Johnson's mother and his stepfather worked to support the household so that John and his half-sister were clothed and fed, and, simultaneously, they taught the value of hard work. Johnson said, he was a "working child" (Johnson 1992: 40).

John Johnson pursued his dream of becoming a journalist. In high school, he "majored in journalism with a related interest in civics" (Johnson 1992: 63). Eventually, he became editor of the Wendell Phillips High School paper and sales manager of the school yearbook. Early in his life during teenage years, Johnson "wanted to be a journalist" (Johnson 1992: 62).

Johnson had to find innovative paths to his goals—many of which were shut off to a working-class African American in depression-era America. For instance, Johnson's educational path would have ended by design in eighth grade, as no secondary school existed in Arkansas City for blacks at the time. Because of the economic realities of the depression, the Johnson family was unable to send him to school in nearby Pine Bluff or Little Rock (Johnson 1992: 49). His mother, Gertrude Johnson Williams, who had a third-grade elementary school education, saved her earnings so that she and John could move to Chicago with a relative, where John could attend and graduate from high school. When their savings turned out to be short of what was needed, Gertrude Johnson Williams told her son that "I was going to return to the Arkansas City School and repeat the eighth grade. She didn't want me running wild on the streets, she said. And she didn't want me to get used to a life of menial work. To prevent that, I was going to repeat the eighth grade two, three, four times—as many times as necessary" (Johnson 1992: 52–53). His mother's short-term goal was to keep her son in school and off the streets until she could save enough money to take him to Chicago where education opportunities were better.

The Johnson family trait of thinking innovatively to confront challenges paid off when John completed high school in Chicago a few years later. His drive and ambition propelled him to a position with Supreme Liberty Insurance, one of the largest African American insurance companies of the day (Johnson 1992: 90). One of Johnson's assignments was to produce a newsletter of events affecting blacks across the nation for the company's customers. After realizing that there was an intense demand for such news, Johnson set to work on producing his own magazine, *Negro Digest*. Ever the innovator, Johnson started work on the first issue without a staff, listing only himself in the magazine's masthead.

Perhaps the most innovative episode during this period of Johnson's life was how he was able to secure the loan that made the initial printing of

Negro Digest possible. Rebuffed by several white-owned banks, Johnson discovered that one bank in Chicago would make loans to blacks. However, the bank required collateral of five hundred dollars in order to extend the load. Johnson turned to his family for help, asking his mother who was the dominant force in the household to agree to use her furniture as collateral. In Johnson's words, "For the first time in all the years I'd known her, she balked. . . . For three or four days we prayed together and cried together. Finally, she said, 'I think the Lord wants me to do it'" (Johnson 1992: 117). The rest, of course is history, as comedian Bill Cosby relates: "John Johnson borrowed $500 on his mother's furniture and created a business empire. Every time I see him I ask, 'Did you ever pay your mother back?'" (Johnson 1992: 373). In 2001, Johnson Publishing Company ranked fourth on the *Black Enterprise* Industrial/Service 100, with sales of over four hundred million dollars (Black Enterprise Research 2002).

John H. Johnson's example demonstrated how working-class black families, burdened by the pressure of economic constraint and racism, find ways to pursue their goals and dreams by creatively crafting methods to challenge the circumstances that confront them as they strive to be successful. This adaptive response by working-class families is in contrast to affluent or middle-class blacks, who often find success by conforming to societal-established goals and methods for the attainment of success.

In "The Black Family and Social Class," Willie elaborates upon the innovative styles and ways of life of black working-class people:

> Black working class families tend to be larger families, consisting of several children. . . . There is some indication that the size of the family is a source of pride for the parents. The bearing and the rearing of the children are considered to be an important responsibility, so much so that black working-class parents make great personal sacrifices for their families. They tend to look upon children as their unique contribution to society, a contribution they are unable to make through the work roles of parents that at best are semi-skilled.
>
> Cohesion within the black working-class family results not so much from understanding and tenderness shown by one another as from the joint and heroic effort to stave off adversity. Without the income of either parent or contributions of children from part-time employment, the family would topple back into poverty.
>
> Parents in black working-class families are literate but have limited formal education. Most have completed elementary school but may be high school dropouts. Seldom do any have more than a high school education. This is the educational level they wish their children to achieve, although some families hope that one or two of the smarter children in their brood will go on to college. The jobs they wish for their children are those that require only a high school or junior college education, like work as a secretary, nurse, mechanic, or factory worker.
>
> Racial discrimination, on the one hand, and insufficient education, on the other, have teamed up to delimit the employment opportunities for black working-class

families. Their mobility from rural to urban areas and from South to North usually has been in search for a better life. Families tend to be attracted to a particular community because of the presence of other relatives who sometimes provided temporary housing.

One sacrifice that the members of black working-class families have made so as to pull out of and stay beyond the clutches of poverty is to give up on doing things as a family. Long working hours sometimes on two jobs leave little time for the father to interact with family members. In some households, the husband works during the daytime and the wife works during the evening hours. In other families, children work up to twenty hours a week after school and on weekends. These kinds of work schedules mean that the family as a unit is not able to share meals together, except possibly on Sunday.

Black working-class parents boast of the fact that their children have food and have not been in trouble with the police. They also have a strong sense of morality that emphasizes "clean living." The home that some families own is part of their claim to respectability. The owned home is one blessing that can be counted. It is a haven from the harsh and sometimes unfriendly world.

Cooperation for survival is so basic in black working-class families that relationships between husband and wife take on a semi-egalitarian character. Each knows that his or her destiny is dependent upon the actions of the other. Within the family, however, husbands and wives tend to have assigned roles, although in time of crisis, these roles can change.

Many working class families are—households moving out of poverty into respectability; households that emphasize mobility, goal and purpose; households committed to making a contribution to society by raising and maintaining a family of good citizens. This, of course, involves a struggle. But the struggle may be a function of the ending of good times rather than the overcoming of adversity. A black working-class family may be of a lower income family on its way up or a middle income household on its way down. A middle income family beset with illness, for example, could slip into the working class status due to reduction in income and the requirement for change in style of living. How often this happens, we do not know. It does occur often enough to keep the working class from becoming a homogenous lot. For this and other reasons, one should not expect to find a common philosophical orientation for all working class. (Willie 1974: 50–60)

Contemporary studies have reinforced many earlier findings. Working-class mothers and fathers have consequently continued to display egalitarian characteristics in their households. In their 1983 study of well-functioning black working-class families, psychiatrists Jerry M. Lewis and John G. Looney reported, "families rated as most competent demonstrated shared parental leadership" (Lewis and Looney 1983: 48). Lewis and Looney acknowledge that not all black working-class families utilize an egalitarian leadership style. "Our findings," they said, "emphasize [that] equal power [in] the marital relationship . . . [is] characteristic [of] the most competent families. Strongly skewed or conflicted marital relationships are characteristic or the least competent families, but not of the sample as a whole" (Lewis and Looney 1983: 140). Robert Hill's research on black families provides further confirmation of egalitarian trends: "Husbands in many black families perform various household tasks, such as cooking, child care, laundering, etc. Clearly, black wives share work responsibilities since they are in the paid labor force in two-thirds of black couples" (Hill, 1999: 109).

The parents in egalitarian, black, working-class families focus strongly on childrearing. In Ramona Denby's analysis of black family preservation, she stated, "A second component of the African American approach to childrearing that has maintained the family unit and is worthy of emulation is the high value placed on children" (Denby 1996: 149). She goes further to explain that African American families often view their offspring as their contribution to society (Denby 1996: 149). While Lewis and Looney did not specifically focus on childrearing in their research on well-functioning, black, working-class families, the authors stated that they "were impressed with the firm but supportive and understanding push of children toward responsible autonomy. The concern about keeping children busy in meaningful activities was particularly apparent in the most competent families" (Lewis and Looney 1983: 134–135).

The example of Gertrude Johnson Williams, the mother of publishing magnate John H. Johnson, vividly illustrates his point. Gertrude Johnson Williams emphasized the value of hard work and education to her son, and invested her future in following his dream as a publisher, with astonishing returns. Granted, most children of working-class black families do not experience financial and professional success to the extent that John H. Johnson did, it is hard to imagine that other proud working-class parents are any less proud of their offspring or less willing to contribute to their children's future.

Educational attainment continues as a theme emphasized by working-class parents. Lewis and Looney found that for black working-class students, education is the path toward better and higher paying jobs after high school "and a better standard of living" (Lewis and Looney 1983: 97).

Another example from the life of John H. Johnson offers an illustration of the black working class equating scholastic progress with employment opportunity. While his performance and promise as a high school student earned Johnson entry into the University of Chicago, he also worked part-time at the Supreme Liberty Life Insurance Company. The work was so engrossing that Johnson later dropped out of college. In his autobiography, he relates, "my real school from 1936–1941 was the university of Supreme Life" (Johnson 1992: 87–88). Though he valued education—and was a good student—Johnson's concern was with education that he could apply directly to his work.

Working-class blacks are hopeful people who believe that "by hook or by crook" their innovative strategies will open ways to overcome or reduce adversity. Lewis and Looney discovered that families in their study expressed little feelings about racial discrimination in their lives. "They seemed to accept that being black meant they had an extra barrier to success because of racial discrimination, but that the barrier could be overcome, particularly by the youngsters in these families" (Lewis and Looney 1983: 128). Black working-class families are acutely aware of the implications of racism and discrimination—however, they have concluded that by working smarter, harder, and innovatively (a method that the business world has labeled "thinking outside the box"), they too can share in the rewards inherent in American society.

John H. Johnson explains this philosophy in a chapter entitled "The Advantage of the Disadvantage." He recounts, "it was worse than useless in that day to grind our teeth and curse racism" (Johnson 1992: 51). His attitude toward impediment due to race is embodied in this dictum: "there's an advantage in every disadvantage, and a gift in every problem" (Johnson 1992: 49). In fact, the impediments of racism led to one of Johnson's most lucrative business ventures. Black models complained to Johnson that they were unable to find cosmetics that complemented their skin tones. When Johnson attempted to convince cosmetics companies to create products for black women, they refused. Thinking creatively, Johnson decided to establish a cosmetics company to serve black women. Today, consumers are familiar with the Fashion Fair line of cosmetics due to Johnson's innovative solution to the discrimination he encountered.

Home ownership remains a goal that many families pursue. In Lewis and Looney's research study, fifteen of eighteen families resided in homes that they were purchasing. There was diversity in the neighborhoods in which the houses were located, with some in lower middle-class communities and others in very poor communities. The researchers discovered that families, while poor, often maintained clean, well-manicured homes, though this was not universally the case (Lewis and Looney 1983: 43). The fact that a majority of these families were purchasing homes indicates the desire of many black families to fulfill the American dream of home ownership, despite the considerable obstacles to this goal.

The immediate needs of the family create a barrier to community involvement for working-class black families. Even if family members have an interest, the collective work of maintaining a household, raising children, and assisting the elderly often prevents sustained civic involvement from taking place.

One pillar of community support for black families is the black church, which represents more than a spiritual base for its members. Brashears and Roberts noted that the significance of the church is correlated to its position in the black community as an institution founded, funded, and operated by blacks, and that leadership opportunities exist in the church which are not accessible to its members in the larger community (Brashears and Roberts 1996: 183).

In Robert Hill's analysis of the religious orientation in black families, he cites a National Urban League survey reporting that middle-income blacks were more likely to belong to a church and attend church on a weekly basis (Hill 1999: 137). Willie's 1985 study had findings about church attendance that were similar to those of Hill. While about half of both middle-class and low-income black families attended church weekly, only a third of working-class black families attended that frequently (Willie 1985: 296). We suspect that the lower figure for regular church attendance among working-class families is due to their work life. Willie's 1985 study found that "work is a consuming experience in most working-class black households. . . . There is little leisure time available and almost no involvement with community organizations. . . . [Working-class] families keep very much to themselves because there simply is not enough time to work as hard as they do, fulfill basic family obligations, and then reach out and relate to the community" (Willie 1985: 156).

LOW-INCOME REBELS

We use the concept rebel to characterize low-income black families in the spirit that it was used by the esteemed black educator Benjamin Elijah Mays as the title for his autobiography *Born to Rebel* (1971).

Mays said that in Greenwood County, South Carolina, in which he lived as a boy, "black was black and white was white and never the twain did meet except in an inferior-superior relationship." For Mays, this was a relationship that he "never sought, cherished, or endured" (Mays 1971: 7–8). Thus, he characterized his childhood that involved working in the field on a tenant farm that his father cultivated for a white landowner as a "life . . . of frustration and doubt," because he aspired to "walk the earth with dignity and pride[,] . . . to achieve, to accomplish, to be 'somebody'" (Mays 1971: 35).

Mays hated the injustices and brutalities heaped upon black people (Mays 1971: vii). He rebelled: first by leaving the farm and going to school, despite his father's objections (Mays 1971: 36); and second, by leaving the South and enrolling in Bates College in Maine against his friends' advice. He did these things, he said, to find himself. Although he never accepted his assigned status in the segregated South, he knew he had to prove his worth and his ability. Mays believed that if he could compete in New England and "with the . . . Yankee," he would have "prima facie evidence that [black people] were not inferior" (Mays 1971: 50). This is the way that Mays rebelled against poverty and the racially oppressive South into which he was born.

Mays acknowledges that there are other ways of rebelling. He observed that some "young black Americans have made great contributions to improve human relations through sit-ins, boycotts, and demonstrations" (Mays, 1971: vii), and that other "young [black] people dropout of school and become delinquent; they see no hope, and some take to rioting" (Mays 1971: viii). All of these are forms of rebelling against a social system that does not support and sustain all of its members.

An example of violent rebellion is the Los Angeles riots of 1993. This incident was precipitated in part by police brutality toward African Americans and the decision by white suburban jurors who found four police officers not guilty of police brutality. Blacks interpreted this decision as a failure of the justice system.

In developing a more adequate social psychology of personal growth, Gordon Allport stated that we must conceptualize personality as a "process of becoming . . . as well [as] a disposition to realize [one's] possibilities" (Allport 1955: 27). He concluded that "it is a limitation of current theories of socialization that they . . . tend to define [it] exclusively in terms of conformity, and not also in terms of creative becoming" (Allport 1955: 35), such as that manifested in the rebellious way of life of Benjamin Mays, who refused to be constrained by the limitations of the environment into which he was born.

Rene DuBos sees the rebel as necessary and essential. "As long as there are rebels in our midst," he states, "there is reason to hope that our societies can be saved" (DuBos 1968: 5). He applauds resistance by young people of some of our social values that tend to dehumanize people (DuBos 1968: 5). Alexander H. Leighton has discussed conflict and disruption as symptoms of social disorganization that, at the same time, may be signs of the repair process (Leighton 1946: 333). He advised institutional agencies to spend less energy "trying to stop the repair process" and more energy on "guiding it in the direction that will be . . . least painful to all concerned" (Leighton 1946: 333).

This discussion helps us to understand the value to our society of rebellious low-income black families. They, like Benjamin Mays and some young people in contemporary times, "cannot have an easy conscience when they know that a better life is a cosmic imperative" (Cook 1971: xviii), and also a possibility. As you may recall from the Mertonian schema reported in chapter 1, low-income black families not only reject the existing goals and methods of society that have closed the door of opportunity and brought harm to them, they advocate alternative goals and methods that, possibly, may better fulfill their needs and those of others. Thus, the rebellious activities of low-income black families, if properly understood and effectively responded to, could make an ethical contribution to the mainstream macrosocial organization of our society. The most important fact about low-income black families is their low-income status; it forces them to make a number of clever, ingenious, and sometimes foolish arrangements to exist. These range from extended households, consisting of several generations under one roof, to taking in boarders or foster children for pay.

These are some additional characteristics frequently found among poor black families:

> Boyfriend-girlfriend relationships between adults often assume some parental functions when children are involved, while the participants maintain their autonomy unfettered by marital bonds. Because every penny counts, poor households often do whatever they must do to bring money in. Conventional practices of mate-selection may be set aside for expedient arrangements that offer the hope of a livable existence.
>
> More often than not, a low-income household does not receive public welfare payments.
>
> Black low-income families learn to live with the contingency. They expect little but hope for more.
>
> Men and women become sexually involved but are afraid to entrust their futures to each. There is much disappointment. The parents in broken families often have broken spirits—too broken to risk a new disappointment. For this reason, black lower-class parents often appear to be uncommitted to anyone or to anything, when in actuality they are afraid to trust.
>
> Movement is constant as if one were afraid to stay put and settle down. Jobs, houses, and cities are changed; so are spouses and boyfriends and girlfriends. Unemployment is a constant specter. . . .
>
> Marriage may occur at an early age. . . . sometimes, the first child is born before the first marriage. Others tend to come in rapid succession. Some families have as many as eight or more children, while other are smaller.
>
> When the burdens of child care, illness, and unemployment strike at the same time, they often are overwhelming. Drinking, gambling, and other escape behavior may increase. A fragile love is shattered, and the man in the house moved out, no longer able to take it. One more failure is experienced.
>
> The parents in black lower-class families [tend to be] grade school or high school dropouts. Neither spouse has more education than the other. Thus, parents in low-income families sometimes hold themselves up to their children as failures, as negative images of what not to do. There is only limited ability to give guidance concerning what ought to be done. Thus, children are advised not to marry early, not to drop out of school, and not to do this and not to do that. There is admonition but little concrete effort at prevention.
>
> Scapegoating is a common way of explaining deviant behavior in children. Juvenile delinquency may be attributed to the disreputable parent.
>
> Although little love may exist between parents, there is fierce loyalty between mothers and offspring, and between grandmothers and children. The children come first. Mothers will extend every effort to take care of their sons and daughters, even into adulthood. Grandparents are excellent babysitters. . . .
>
> A strong custom of brothers and sisters helping each other exists in the black low-income families. The problem is that siblings are struggling, too. About the

most one can do for the other is share already overcrowded living quarters when a new family member comes to town or when a two-parent family breaks down. The movement from one city to another often is for the purpose of being near kin. There is strong loyalty between siblings and a standing obligation to help.

Religion is important for some low-income [black] families. But for others, it is no more than a delusion. Those who attend church regularly tend to engulf their lives with religion and especially with affirmations about its saving grace and reward system after death. Some shy away from the church as one more disappointing promise that has copped out on the poor without really helping. Black low-income people are seldom lukewarm about religion. They are either all for it or all against it, although the latter are reluctant to deny their children religious experience, just in case there is more to it than was realized.

An increasing number of parents in black low-income families mentioned the armed forces as an employment opportunity for their children. (Willie 1974: 50–60)

To summarize, it is hard for a poor black family to overcome poverty; so much is lined up against it. If illness or unemployment do not drain away resources, there is a high probability that old age will.

The "egalitarian arrangement" seen among middle-class blacks was also present among poor, low-income, two-parent black families; the major difference between the two income groups was the low incidence of this arrangement because of the high proportion of single-parent families among the poor. In the two-parent black families, husbands and fathers often boast of their culinary arts. Food preparation is not limited to women. Some men are proud to be good cooks.

Improving the socioeconomic status of their family is one goal of family members among poor black people. But more important than this is the achievement of dignity, an idea mentioned early on by Mays that is still a goal among poor black people today. In a previous study, the senior author of this book found that the family goal mentioned more frequently than any other is that of raising respectable children—"offspring who are decent, well behaved and worthy of esteem" (Willie 1985: 228).

While poor black people flail out sometimes and rebel against an indifferent society, their main mission as a people is rescuing and redeeming fallen individuals (Willie 1985: 231). They try to accomplish this mission on their own and with help through the church. Poor black people were particularly pleased when their churches supported the Civil Rights Movement, which was designed to rescue the perishing and care for the fallen.

"The needs of individuals take precedence" (Willie 1985: 231). The care and concern exhibited by poor black families for individual members who are "down and out" is similar in some ways to the interests of the white middle class that, according to Willie's 1985 study, "will do whatever is necessary to protect and promote the autonomy of individuals" (Willie 185: 116). Carla

O'Connor's review of professional literature reveals similar findings that many poor African-Americans believe in the American dream and that personal aspirations may be achieved by way of hard work and effort. But they also know that external factors constrain their upward mobility (O'Connor 2000: 108), and, despite their best efforts, hard work has not always led to fulfillment of their goals.

By rebelling against an indifferent society, poor black people exercise veto power. The alternative methods and goals they introduce to make circumstances and conditions of life more tolerable for them is called, by Hyman Rodman, the stretching of common values rather than repudiation of them (Rodman 1971).

Poor black people cease cooperating with the society at large and rebel if necessary when they determine that "the cards are stacked against them." An example is the law pertaining to cocaine usage. Drug offenders who use crack cocaine receive longer sentences than drug offenders who use powder cocaine; crack cocaine is most frequently used by blacks and powder cocaine is most frequently used by whites. Laws like this that, in effect, mandates different punishments by race for use of an illegal common substance such as cocaine has been labeled by sociologist Robert Hill as "institutional racism" (Hill 1999: 22, 24). While poor black people may not have a fancy label like "institutional racism" to identify the punishment and injustice, they know that the longer sentence in jail is disproportionately harmful to them compared with whites, and, therefore, they have learned to cease cooperating in their own oppression. Veto is the ultimate resistance available to subdominant people in the community's power structure. Increasingly, poor black people are using it against unjust practices of the society and its institutions.

To summarize, the members of poor black families deny that they are responsible for their lot in life; they do not attribute it to luck or chance but to defects in the operation of the social system. Poor black people perceive society and its institutions as hostile to them and their well-being. Because poor black people have an abiding belief in religion that identifies love as the basic norm of society, and because they know that "love and justice are the same, for justice is love distributed" (Fletcher 1967: 16–17) and believe that "only the end [—the well-being of each person—] justifies the means" (Fletcher 1967: 22), they ask not what they can do for an unjust society but what the system can do for those it has harmed. From the perspective of poor black people, the needs of each individual are important; all else is secondary. We conclude that poor black families practice a more or less pure brand of distributive justice that focuses on the responsibility of the group for the individual.

II

ANALYSES OF BLACK FAMILIES BY SOCIAL CLASS

3

Middle-Class Black Families

THE ALLEN FAMILY CASE STUDY

By Andrew F. Noga

My mother had copied down both the time that Peter and Beverly Allen were expecting me and the directions to their house, since I had not been home to receive Peter's phone call. On a Sunday afternoon in late December I headed for Philadelphia, Pennsylvania. While I knew this area reasonably well because my favorite movie theater is located near the Allens' home, I had never traveled down their street. The drive over was rather uneventful except for the fact that I had left the directions at my parents' house. I drove up to a colonial house with a white picket fence—this was the one piece of information that I remembered. As I rang the doorbell, an older woman came to the door. She assured me that the Allens lived next door. I was proud of myself; I was not lost at all.

Before I rang the Allens' doorbell, I stood on the porch watching a young, black boy tossing around a baseball with two white boys. Each of the boys seemed to be enjoying himself, running around in circles and trying to make diving catches on the soggy front yard. All three boys appeared to be at least ten or eleven years old. As I later discovered, the young black boy was Darren Allen. I introduced myself by extending a warm handshake to Darren and to his two friends and Darren said in a friendly tone that his parents were expecting me.

Peter Allen, the father of the Allen family, came to the door and led me on a circuitous route through the living room back to the kitchen. Upon entering the Allens' house, I noticed several children's games and toys in the front hall. There was an older computer set up in the front room with plenty of disks and other computer paraphernalia strewn around the machine itself. The walls in the front hall looked as if they had not been painted in several years. In the living room, there were a few pictures with Peter, Beverly, and the children. However, there was one picture that stood out among the rest because there was only one individual in the photo. The person was Peter's eldest son, Peter Allen III. Dressed in his cap and gown and holding his diploma, he grinned with a cherubic smile. The picture captured a young man who was visibly ecstatic because the ultimate day had arrived. His father told me that this photo was taken when Peter graduated from Amherst in 1993.

Peter and I finally entered the kitchen where Beverly was waiting for us at the table. She immediately fixed her gaze on my tape recorder and I asked her if taping the interview would make her feel uncomfortable. She never directly addressed my question, but she was quite interested in the course that required this type of in-depth interview. After I spoke about the nature of the course itself and about my reasons for requesting the interview, I sensed that Peter and Beverly felt much more at ease with me and with the overall interviewing process. Beverly walked over to the refrigerator to pour herself a cold beverage and she brought me a glass of water. Sitting down at the table again, Beverly requested that we proceed because she had to leave by 4:30 P.M. with the children for the weekly service at church.

Peter Allen II is a fifty-six-year-old black man who was born in Montgomery, Alabama, and lived there until he was twenty years old. Both of Peter's parents completed undergraduate degrees. Obtaining a college degree was an issue that Peter's parents constantly stressed with their children. Peter's father relocated to Philadelphia by himself for a job in 1945 while Peter's mother and five children remained in Montgomery. A schoolteacher in the Montgomery district, Peter's mother was not willing to forsake her position; moreover, she did not want to take her children away from the support of relatives and friends. Peter completed his high school education at one of Montgomery's public schools. In fact, Peter related to me that on a daily basis he walked three and one-half miles to his high school and returned home by the same route. The problem that Peter experienced with this daily journey was not the length of the route but the fact that he had to walk by the neighborhood high school which was located at the end of his block. Peter was a high school student when the civil rights movement was gaining momentum in the South and, in particular, in Montgomery. He did not want to get involved in the civil rights movement in Montgomery because he feared for his own safety and physical well-being. His family expected him to "act in an educated way." Peter continued, "Education was the key to getting out, to beating the system." Consequently, Peter opted to relocate to the Philadelphia area in 1962 in order to attend college. During his undergraduate years,

Peter lived with his father who was still working in Philadelphia. Peter enrolled at Temple University where he graduated in 1966 with a degree in mathematics. Conducting laboratory research for a noted dentist was Peter's first "real" job. Peter worked for the dentist the next three decades at two different locations in Philadelphia. When funding ceased for the research project two years ago, Peter was left without a job. He still does not have a full-time job, but he continues to look for a position that really interests him. Although Peter does not draw an income from full-time employment, he does earn a regular income from investments that he made while still employed.

Peter first married in the mid-1970s. Peter and his first wife, Emily, had one child together—Peter Allen III. This marriage lasted less than a decade, yet Emily still keeps in contact with their son even though Peter retained custody of him. While Peter, the father, no longer keeps in contact with Emily, he does see her at special occasions including their son's high school and college graduations. Peter harbors no resentment towards his first wife. Indeed, Emily contributed most of the financial resources so that their son was able to attend an academically rigorous, private high school in Philadelphia. Emily currently resides in Virginia, moving there after residing in Detroit for many years.

Beverly Allen, Peter's second wife, is a black woman in her mid-forties who grew up in the Philadelphia metropolitan area. While Beverly says that her children consider themselves to be "Afro-American," she insists that she and Peter are "black." She went on to say: "Peter and I are the older generation. I'd say we are black because of our age. Also, the experiences that I have had. This answer really reflects a difference in age."

Beverly is one of five children in her family of origin. Raised in a primarily black neighborhood in Philadelphia, Beverly has always attended public schools. After completing high school, she attended Temple University where she received an undergraduate degree in education. Beverly returned to Temple University to pursue an M.Ed. with a concentration in educational administration, and she graduated four years later.

Beverly enjoyed her first, professional position as a nursing administrator. She worked at the same hospital in Philadelphia where Peter worked, and they met each other there. They married in 1981. At a certain point, Beverly grew tired of hospital work and decided that she wanted to use her undergraduate training in education. Beverly taught her first two years in the Philadelphia public school system. In 1989 she accepted a position teaching third grade in a suburban school district. Her decision to move to the district was influenced by two factors: a shorter commute to work and a noticeable salary increase. However, Beverly had more to contend with than she ever anticipated when she accepted the position. Beverly was the first black educator—male or female—hired to teach in the suburban district's elementary system. Beverly has been teaching in the district for eight years now. She reflects on her reasons for teaching there by saying:

> I teach out in the suburbs now because I was raised in the city and I remember not being allowed to go there as a child. So I wanted to make a difference. Since I was the first black, elementary schoolteacher in the district, and, now, we have more, I know I am making a difference. These little, white children are now growing up knowing that "people are people." It doesn't matter what skin color you have, I know I am making a difference. And my goal is to change the thinking of the children so that, hopefully, they will go home and change the thinking of the parents. There was some initial resistance until the parents got to know me. There was this resistance until they found out what I was doing with their children.

Beverly currently earns a salary in the low 40s for her teaching efforts.

Since both Peter and Beverly have worked throughout most of their marriage, they share many of the chores around the house. When the children were below school age, Peter dropped them off at a day care facility or at the home of Beverly's mother who resided near where Peter was working at the time. In fact, Beverly's mother cared for all three children while they were young. Today, the Allen children have grown up and look after themselves when their parents leave the house for a while.

As stated earlier, Peter Allen III is the son of Peter and Emily. Now twenty-five years old, Peter is a second-year law student at Harvard University. He hopes to focus his attention on corporate law and desires to work in either New York City or Washington, D.C. After graduating from Amherst College in 1993, Peter received a fellowship to Cambridge University where he studied for the next two years. When Peter III has extended vacations or breaks from school, he always stays with Peter, Beverly, and his siblings. He enjoys a close relationship with his maternal grandparents and attends religious services with them when he returns to Philadelphia.

Ricky L. Allen, age fifteen, is the oldest of Peter and Beverly's three children. A sophomore at one of the city's best high schools, Ricky is a solid student who participates in basketball and swimming. He is not sure about his future plans, but "he is still considering the value of a college education." Ricky rarely, if ever, causes any anxiety for his parents. He is mindful of his responsibilities and chores around the house. Ricky has plenty of friends in the neighborhood; a few joined him at his home during the course of the interview. When speaking about Ricky's friends as well as the other two children's friends, Beverly interjected, "Peter and I don't care what color the children's friends are. We just care that they are good and decent people."

Darren F. Allen, age twelve, is the second of the three children. Swimming and diving are his primary interests; yet, he maintains respectable grades in all of his subjects. When asked about Darren's future goals, Beverly responded, "Darren has told me that he will do whatever it takes to make good money." Although Darren is not a "chronic troublemaker," Beverly quickly pointed out, "Darren sometimes has trouble channeling his energies. Actually, he really stretches our creativity as parents." Darren, like his older brother Ricky, has several friends in the neighborhood with whom he attends school and with whom he plays on the weekends.

Ella A. Allen, age nine and one-half, is a fourth-grade student in elementary school. An avid swimmer like her older brothers, Ella is a very motivated student. After eating a quick snack upon returning home from school, Ella closes her bedroom door and begins working on her nightly studies. Most of her friends are members of her swim team; as a result, she only sees them during practice a few times per week. Ella hopes someday to be a teacher just like her mother.

If there is an incident that involves disciplining a child, whichever parent is present settles the matter promptly. Both parents share equal responsibility in this area of their children's lives. Peter and Beverly feel it "would be unfair to make one parent the bad guy. We love our children and we want them to know that this is *our* house."

The Allen family now lives in suburban Philadelphia, Pennsylvania—a middle- to upper-class suburb. The Allens' neighbors are a mixture of professional families—doctors, dentists, lawyers, and business people. They know "probably twelve families in their neighborhood really well" because of the children's friendships with the children of these families and because of an annual, summer block party "where we really enjoy a day together with all the families in the area." The Allens moved to this neighborhood eight years ago; actually, Beverly found the house and put in the bid without any consultation with Peter. They really like this neighborhood because it is multiracial. Beverly expanded on this thought:

> The togetherness of this community is what really sold me. It really is a together community. There are not any problems in this neighborhood. I feel safe here and so do our kids. That is what is really important to me. I have never had any problems with the families or the kids in the neighborhood. . . . When we decided to move, we did not want an all-black community or an all-white one. We were really looking for a community where our children would experience a variety of people. We also know a lot of people in this neighborhood, maybe thirty or so. Most of them we know because of the kids.

I then asked if there was noticeable police presence in the neighborhood and Beverly assured me that this was the case. However, she immediately added, "The police are always around. Because my children know the police, they see the police as their friends, not as cops. This is the real advantage of having community-policing."

Beverly and Peter have contemplated the possibility of relocating. Atlanta and other southern cities, with the exception of Montgomery, have been discussed, yet both Beverly and Peter remain unsure about the timing of such a move. Besides the fact that the Allens' present neighborhood is a multiracial one, the other factor that influenced the Allens' decision to move to suburban Philadelphia was the renowned school system. Beverly and Peter's three children have always attended public schools and Beverly is most fond of this particular school system:

> The teachers, the instruction, the administration in the schools—we have had to deal with all of them quite a bit. We are really pleased with our school system and the services that it provides. The parents here make the school system reach out to them. The adults in this community are professionals—they want solid educations for their kids, also.

During the week, there is a "considerable amount of activity" in the Allen house. Beverly rises at 6:00 A.M. so that she is able to leave the house by 7:00 A.M. or so. Beverly wakes up Peter and the three children around 6:45 A.M. and quickly drinks a cup of coffee before she leaves. She commutes by car to her school, a commute that only takes thirty minutes because she is heading against traffic. Charged with ensuring that the children eat breakfast, Peter never has a problem accomplishing this task, although each child usually eats alone. When the children are ready to leave, Peter drives all three of them to school. While the children are at school and Beverly is at work, Peter usually works at home on his personal computer. Peter picks up the children after school unless there is swimming practice. In that case, the children walk with their friends to the pool that is not too far from their schools. When the children finally arrive home, Peter explains:

> They have a half-hour respite where they can relax, get something to eat, make a phone call—whatever they want to do before they head off to their own room to study and finish their homework. At 8:30 P.M., they go to bed. There are no late nights in this house.

Peter and Beverly assist all children with any difficulties that they experience with their schoolwork as well as with reviews of vocabulary and spelling. Peter loves to work with the children on math problems, especially algebra and geometry problems. While Peter is helping the children in the afternoon with their studies, Beverly usually returns home from school at 5:00 P.M. She eats a quick bite with Peter; the entire Allen family seldom eats together during the week. Beverly usually spends the next three hours correcting her students' papers, reading for her graduate courses, and helping her own children with their studies. The children do not watch very much television during the week, and, when they do watch, Peter or Beverly try to steer them toward programs airing on PBS such as *Nova* or *Cosmos*. The children retire for the evening at 8:30 P.M. or so. After the children are asleep, Peter and Beverly are able to discuss the day without any interruptions. Also, Peter and Beverly always "keep an eye on the programs on PBS. We really like the shows which are on there, especially the science programs." They usually head off to sleep after they watch the eleven o'clock news.

The weekends are "much less hectic" than the weekdays at the Allen house. On Saturday and Sunday mornings, all of the Allens sleep until at least 9:00 A.M. On Saturdays, Beverly, Peter, and the children take care of their chores for the week. After the house is cleaned and the chores are finished, the children have the rest of the day to themselves. They are free to play with friends, to see a movie, or to just relax at home. Peter often spends Saturday afternoons in the basement where he has fashioned a woodworking shop for himself. Sometimes Peter enjoys reading one of the magazines to which he subscribes: *Woodworking*, *PC*, and *Time*. On Saturday morning, Beverly often cooks several dishes so that the children have prepared dinners during the week. On Saturday afternoons, Beverly concentrates her energies on her graduate courses because she knows that she has limited time during the week. To give herself a break during the afternoon, Beverly reads *Ebony*, the only magazine to which she subscribes. With the entire family at home on Saturday evening, Peter tries to find a movie that is educational and thought-provoking. Occasionally, Peter and Beverly invite some friends over to their house to play cards. This is the one night of the week when the children are allowed to stay up past 8:30 P.M. Peter and Beverly usually permit the children to stay up until 11:00 P.M. on Saturday nights, although the children rarely stay up that late.

On Sunday mornings, Beverly and the three children attend religious services at a nondenominational church that is close to Beverly's mother's home. While Beverly asserted that she and the children are "Methodists," she explained why she and the children attend this nondenominational church: "I made the decision about religion. Peter is not religious. I like to take the children with me because I usually go to church with my mother and my sister. It's good for them to visit with their aunt and grandmother."

After church, Beverly and the children often return to either her sister's house or her mother's house where they talk about family matters and the children spend some time with extended family members. When I asked Beverly if she participated in any other ways at her church, she responded that she does not. However, she quickly said, "Call me, ask me, and I'll do whatever I can." While Beverly and the children are away from the house, Peter reads *The Sunday Philadelphia Inquirer*. This is the only day on which the Allens receive the paper because Peter and Beverly "don't have time to read the daily paper." When they return from visiting relatives, the children play in the afternoon with friends. Beverly, meanwhile, prepares the evening dinner. Sunday is the one day that the entire Allen family eats together. This meal always occurs at 5:00 P.M. and every member of the family is expected to be present. After dinner, Beverly heads to the study in order to complete her weekly lesson plans. This is always a lengthy project, one that usually keeps Beverly occupied until she heads off to bed at 11:00 P.M.

Peter and Beverly try to plan special family outings. The entire Allen family with the exception of Peter III vacations together on a yearly basis. Beverly selects the location, with Florida and the beaches of South Carolina being the more recent excursions. During most summers, Peter's relatives from Montgomery travel to Philadelphia to see the Allens. Peter's siblings bring their families so that the children can play together and see the Philadelphia "Phillies" baseball team play. Also, Beverly enjoys taking her children during the summer to the various museums in Philadelphia. Peter, Beverly, and the children spend much time during summer months at the community pool located at the end of their street. The Allen children swim in a club team that practices there; many of their friends participate in activities at the pool.

Peter noted that this past year has been a difficult one for him personally with the death of his father. While Peter regrets the fact that his children will no longer be able to visit their grandfather, he is especially upset because his father was the sole reason that Peter journeyed to Philadelphia in the first place.

When I asked Beverly and Peter what their family was attempting to accomplish in life, Beverly did not hesitate to answer: "We are trying to raise kind-hearted, gentle beings who are truly colorblind, who have a distinct pride in their ethnicity."

At this point I felt that I had received plenty of data and I was pretty happy with the flow of the interview. However, I wanted to ask one more question and I did. The question was this: Is it difficult raising a black family in America today? Beverly sat back in her chair and thought for a minute. Then, she responded:

> There is a disparaging view of black males today because many are dead or are in jail, unfortunately. But, that is where the church comes in. Most women who are raising their children as single parents are involved in their church. In the church are the deacons and ministers who are the male role models. I find it very difficult to raise black children today. I hate the music, the suggestive music. There is only so much you can do to get around it especially when you have a fifteen-year-old son who buys his own CDs and puts on his earphones and tunes you out. Television is a little bit better, but not that much better. Yes, we have our shows, but if it is not on WB, you're not going to see it because, at least, they have quality black shows which don't make us look like idiots. . . . Also, I don't like these bourgeois blacks who forget from whence they came.

Finally, as Beverly checked her watch and realized that she needed to pick up her mother for the 5:00 P.M. church service, she rushed to put on her coat.

She called upstairs to the children and they headed out to the car. Before Beverly left, she made sure to tell me that this year the Allen family is celebrating Kwanzaa, a feast that will take place from December 26th through January 1st. Beverly decided that the whole Allen family should celebrate the holiday after researching the premise behind the celebration three years ago for her students. When Beverly finally finished relating the significance of each day of the celebration to me, she asked Peter to warm up a plate of her special, black-eyed peas for me.

I left the Allen home with great respect for the efforts that Beverly and Peter Allen make on behalf of their children.

THE HART FAMILY CASE STUDY

By Magdalena Martinez

I visited the Hart family one December evening. As I approached their home I could see the Harts' natural Christmas tree from outside. Although I had never visited the Hart home before, the view into their home from outside gave me a sense of warmth and hospitality. I rang the doorbell and was greeted by Reginald Hart. I first met Reginald eight months ago. Before taking me any further into his home, he explained that everyone that enters the house must take off their shoes at the entrance. He said it was a family habit they developed since the children were small to keep the home clean. I took my shoes off and followed him into the kitchen. In the kitchen was his "lovely wife" Sherry. Reginald often refers to her as his "lovely wife." Sherry and I sat at the kitchen table while Reginald sat on the family couch with the sports channel on. Although Reginald was not seated at the table with Sherry and me, he was close enough to actively participate in the interview. Reginald also kept the TV on mute during the duration of our interview. I could hear the children upstairs talking and watching TV. They remained upstairs until the conclusion of our interview. At that time, Reginald and Sherry called their three children and introduced them to me. The Hart family consists of mother, father, three children (two sons and one daughter), and a dog.

The Family

Reginald was born in Georgia. Reginald comes from a military family, as such he and his siblings traveled and moved often within the United States and internationally while they were growing up. Reginald considers himself African American. Reginald has two other brothers. Reginald is in his mid-forties and the second oldest of his siblings. Reginald's father was in the service and traveled around the world. His mother was a homemaker.

Reginald's father completed high school only, while Reginald's mother completed two years of college. Reginald completed his undergraduate studies at Armstrong State and earned his master's in Public Administration at Georgia State University. Following in the steps of his father, Reginald recently retired from a twenty-year career in the military. He retired as an Army major. He currently is employed as a personnel analyst with Phoenix, Arizona, in the department of Human Resources. His responsibilities range from training and development for management, disciplinary hearings, and internal consulting on various personnel issues. He has been employed by the city of Phoenix for nearly a year.

Sherry was born in Alabama and raised in Salinas, California. She considers herself African American. Her father has a doctorate in social service administration and is retired; her mother has a master's degree and taught elementary school. Her parents divorced when she was seven or eight years old. Sherry has three siblings, two brothers, and one sister. She is in her early forties and the third oldest of her siblings. Sherry completed her undergraduate studies in sociology and her master's in education at Georgia State. She has served as an elementary school counselor for the past two years with the local school district. Prior to her current position, she worked for the District of Columbia school district.

Reginald and Sherry first met in Salinas, California, when Reginald was stationed by the Army in that area. The couple had been married for twenty years at the time of this interview. The Hart family has resided in Arizona for two years. Prior to living in Phoenix, the Hart family lived in Silver Spring, Maryland. As a military family, the Harts moved every two to three years within the United States and internationally.

The couple's oldest child is Simon. He is sixteen and is in the tenth grade and attends the local, public high school. Simon actively participates in sports. He plays football and basketball. Simon has an attention deficit disorder, which was diagnosed while he was in second grade. Sherry explained that once the disorder was identified, Simon progressed well until the fifth and sixth grades. That year, the family moved three times because of Reginald's military assignments. In the sixth grade, Simon became interested in music. As a result, his grades improved. Sherry shared more information about Simon:

> He has to relate to something to be motivated and do well. While in middle school in Indiana, he was very motivated by the bandleader. He played clarinet two years. Then we came to Phoenix. Now he is an athlete and plays baseball and basketball. His grades are average ranging from B's to C's.

Currently, Simon does not work although he wants to. Reginald didn't mind him working because he feels Simon "needs a job to develop a sense of ownership and responsibility." Sherry was against the idea of him working because she feels he has too much on his plate with school and sports.

Martin is the second oldest child and is twelve years old. He is in the seventh grade and attends the local public school. Martin has a processing deficit or learning disability, which was diagnosed while he was in second grade. Initially, Sherry had to push the school district to examine him. Sherry stated that Martin was not having a tremendous amount of difficulty in school but enough to make him feel different, so she persisted in requesting that he should be tested. In the third grade he was placed in a resource class. Martin has not had any problem since then. He is now attending mainstream classes. His average grades range from A's to B's.

Trinette is the youngest child and the only daughter. She is nine years old and is in the third grade. "Trinette is very bright," described Sherry. She has no problems in school; however, she did start school late because of a state law that did not allow students to enroll until the age of five. Therefore, her mother homeschooled her. Trinette knew her alphabet, numbers, colors, and was reading by the time she was in kindergarten. The school district suggested that she be placed in a gifted program. Sherry and Reginald decided against it because of their fear that she could lose the enjoyment of learning. As an educator, Sherry has seen many unsuccessful gifted programs. Because the family has moved often, Trinette has been in three different schools, but this has not affected her grades. She is a straight-A student. However, because Trinette started school late, her classmates are usually younger than she is. Trinette has experienced some problems due to the relocation process, but, explains Sherry, these have not affected her grades.

Their Home and Community

The Harts and their children live in a middle- to upper-class neighborhood in Phoenix, Arizona. About one-third of the family's income comes from Reginald's military retirement. The two-story house has four bedrooms and a large living, dining, and family room. There are a total of nine rooms in the house and a swimming pool in the backyard for the summer, hot, desert days. They purchased the house two years ago when Reginald retired from the military. I asked the Harts if they lived in military housing during Reginald's service. Interestingly, the Hart family avoided living in military houses as much as possible. Instead, they purchased a home almost every time they moved. Reginald wanted his family to live in a civilian neighborhood. He stated that his job was on base, but once he was home, he was Reginald not Major Hart.

The Harts know about five to ten families in the neighborhood. Their children are very popular and always have friends and schoolmates over at the house. Sherry likes the neighborhood but does not like that the next-door neighbor, he does not attend to his yard and has old vehicles in it that he works on. Reginald loves the neighborhood because the commute to and from work is fast and easy. The neighborhood is safe and comfortable. The Harts have thought about moving, not because they don't like their home, but because they are used to moving so often. They purchased the house with a five-year plan in mind, that they would live in the house at least five years and then upgrade to a better home. They have lived in this house for almost three years. The neighborhood is a mixed population with Hispanic, Asian, Indian, and Greek families. The Harts are, however, the only African American family.

The Harts home is beautifully decorated with Japanese and African American art and pictures. Hanging above the fireplace is a poster of all the African American fraternities and sororities. Sherry explained what organization each figure represented.

Family Decisions and Structure

Sherry and the children are Catholic. Reginald is Methodist. The children attend bible study classes regularly. Sherry and the children attend church once or twice a month. Occasionally, Reginald will join them and is considering becoming Catholic.

Family decisions and responsibilities are somewhat shared equally among the couple. For example, both help the children with their homework; however, because Sherry is the educator in the family, she will often help more than Reginald. Because of Reginald's military career, Sherry often took a majority of the responsibilities and continues to take many of these responsibilities, such as taking care of sick children, making dinner, assigning chores, deciding what school and church the family attends, and talking to the children's teachers. During the interview Reginald seemed a bit upset when Sherry responded that she usually goes and talks to the teachers. Sherry clarified that both of them attend open houses during the school year; however, Sherry usually visits the teachers regarding academic issues of the children. The couple will discuss and decide on other issues and major purchases for the family, such as the house and the number of children to have. The couple also discusses career options with their children. Both parents encourage higher education for their children. The children do not get an allowance, but the couple is considering inaugurating this practice.

Prior to Reginald's retirement, the Army would decide where the family lived. However, during moves, the couple would almost always discuss the home they would purchase. Once Reginald retired, the couple decided to move to the state where the first spouse received a job offer. Sherry received an offer in Arizona and the family decided to move as planned. In deciding what house to purchase, the family tried a different approach. One weekend Sherry went to Arizona and photographed homes that she liked. Once the pictures were developed, Reginald and the children decided what house they would purchase.

The couple is registered to vote and belongs to the Democratic political party. They talk about issues but not platforms. They seldom talk about how each spouse will vote. The family receives news from television, online news, and the local newspaper. Reginald subscribes to *Golf Digest* and *PC World* magazines. Sherry occasionally receives *Ebony* and *Redbook*. She admits to subscribing to these magazines when her children sell them as part of school fundraisers. The children receive *Highlights* and *Nickelodeon*. Trinette likes to read Beverly Cleary books while Martin prefers *Goosebumps*, a children's horror story series. Sherry loves to read science fiction books and usually reads every day no matter how tired she is. She reads about five books a month. Trinette and Sherry read the most in the family. Trinette spends a lot of time writing in her journal as well.

Reginald spends about three to five hours a day watching TV, usually sports. Sherry likes to watch TV on Fridays and Sundays; during the week, she watches the news. She watches science fiction shows like *The X-Files*. She will usually watch TV about one and one-half hours a day. The couple monitors what the children watch on TV. The children also like science fiction shows. They watch MTV and Nickelodeon. The children watch TV an average of two hours a day.

The family belongs to few social organizations except church and sports for the children. Reginald is a member of the Omega Psi Phi Fraternity and a few professional organizations. Sherry belongs to several professional organizations related to her career. Martin and Simon both play basketball or baseball and Trinette has taken gymnastics. The couple expressed an interest in enrolling her in gymnastics again. Reginald described his family "as not too active but instead like to keep to themselves." When the couple was in the service, they had a stronger support group and were involved in other activities. Currently, they are adjusting to a civilian lifestyle.

The Harts are a military family and as such they are able to adapt easily to new environments, including states, schools, and jobs. Prior to Reginald's retirement from the Army, the couple and children did not mind the moving, primarily because Reginald and Sherry made every effort to make it seem like a family vacation every time they had to move. Real family vacations usually include visiting family members. Occasionally, Sherry will visit her mother by herself and Reginald will go golfing elsewhere with his brother.

The family has adapted very well to Arizona. Sherry admitted that this is the first time the children have attended such racially diverse schools. Prior to living in Nevada, the couple had the ability to place their children in any school they wished. Sherry shared this experience:

> We wanted the kids to have the best education; so most of the time they attended affluent schools. But here, it's different. There's a difference in the population. It has been good for the kids. They feel better seeing and socializing with more blacks, Hispanics, and Asians. This was always an issue when they attended affluent schools. In one case, Simon was the only black student. Students always wanted to touch his hair. Simon came home and told me. I immediately went to the school and told the teacher that my child was not an animal to be petted. The teacher tried to explain that the children were curious. I told her there are other ways to educate children about different races.

The Hart's do not have extended family members that live in Arizona so they have to rely on themselves. Reginald explained that this has always been the case for his family, because they traveled so often. The couple will talk to family members about every three to four days. Reginald shared:

> It has always been only us; we have learned to rely on each other because of my military career. We have moved fifteen different times within the eighteen years of marriage. We are private people and comfortable with each other. We don't entertain much or go out. Except for Fridays. Sherry and I will have a date. We will usually go out and enjoy ourselves without the kids. We come back home early about 8:30 P.M.

Other social activities include going to the movies. Reginald doesn't like going to movies; but Sherry usually goes with the children. Sherry stated that the children spend more time with her than with Reginald. Reginald likes to golf and is usually golfing on the weekends.

On the weekend Reginald leaves the house for the golf course around 6:30 A.M. and is back by 11:30 A.M. Sherry gets up at 8:30 A.M. and works, researches her family background, plays games, or chats on the computer. Martin and Trinette get up about 9:00 A.M. or 10:00 A.M. Family members clean and complete their chores first. Trinette usually spends time writing in her journal. Simon wakes up about 11:00 A.M. Once Reginald arrives home, the family will usually go on doing the same thing, whether it's using the computer, reading, playing sports, watching TV, or listening to the radio. Reginald shared, "We are not so structured; everyone does one's own thing. We are homebodies. We don't like to go places." Reginald and his sons will usually watch sports on TV. Sherry said jokingly, "I'm losing my boys to sports." Reginald said his sons are comfortable when he is home and stated that they are talking to him more as they have gotten older, especially Simon. In the evening, the family will have dinner together.

Describing the typical weekday, Sherry jokes and says, "We run and scream." Reginald and Sherry will get up about 5:30 A.M. and start getting ready for work. Simon will be picked up by the school bus around 6:30 A.M. Martin will usually walk to school, since it is only a few blocks from their home. Sherry will take Trinette to school. The family eats breakfast in shifts before leaving for work or school. Sherry gets off from work at 3:30 P.M. and will pick up Simon from school after football or basketball practice. She will pick up Martin and Trinette as well. Sherry is home with the children about 4:00 P.M. She doesn't go back out after 4:00 P.M. unless she needs to stop at the grocery store. The couple usually does grocery shopping once a week at the local military base. Reginald gets home around 5:30 P.M. or 6:30 P.M. At that time, the family will have dinner. After dinner the children do their chores and then their homework. Reginald and Sherry will assist them if they need help, otherwise they will relax and watch the news. The children are usually in bed by 9:00 P.M. to 10:00 P.M. The couple will usually go to bed soon after their children.

Discipline

Both Reginald and Sherry discipline the children, although Sherry disciplines more often because she is home more than Reginald.

The children have not had any problems with law enforcement. Sherry mentioned an incident Simon had when he was in the first grade. He and other boys were throwing rocks from a hill.

The children look out for each other outside the home, but usually argue with each other at home. Trinette and Martin will usually argue the most because they are the youngest. Simon is a regular sixteen-year-old who does not have any disciplinary problems at school or outside of school. Reginald described him as "a good kid."

Remembering Good Times

Sherry shared that they are most of the time content with the family. Reginald enjoys the holidays because the entire family gets a break from school and work. This is family time. The couple also enjoys their children's accomplishments, such as Simon making the basketball and football team. The entire family will attend the children's sports events.

Family Adaptation during Difficult Times

For difficult times or emergencies, the couple turns to each other and, if need be, to extended family such as parents, brothers, or sisters. Sherry described a difficult time for the family:

> When we had to move from the West Coast to the Midwest, we [Sherry and Reginald] were separated for a long period of time, about four or five months. This

was the first move we had planned and everything went wrong. That's when Simon was having problems in school. We had to stay in military quarters, which were very small. I was then told I had to move out, so I had to find an apartment within a few days. The children were small. This move was a complete nightmare. We were finally able to settle in and buy our home, but during those months everything that could go wrong, went wrong.

Another example of a difficult time is when Martin was removed from class when the family lived in the Midwest. Sherry explained that it was Black History Month and all of the black children were taken out of class to talk about Martin Luther King Jr. and black history. Martin came home and asked if he had done something bad. Sherry asked why, and Martin explained that all the children were taken in small groups to talk about him and he felt the teachers were being secretive. Sherry immediately went to talk to the teacher. The teacher attempted to justify why only the black children were taken out. Sherry told the teacher her children knew about Black History Month and suggested that the other children needed to be educated together, as one group, not in isolation.

Family Goals and Expectations

Reginald shared that he would like his family to be comfortable and the children to be responsible. Sherry added that she wanted her children to be strong and prepared. I asked her to explain in more detail.

> I want my children to have a strong character and for them to know who they are, no matter what obstacles they run into. My boys are black males. We know there are laws but the reality is there is overt racism in our society. I want them to be successful and do what they want to do, and not be stopped because of it. Trinette will probably face more sexism than racism because she is a black female. But by being prepared and having a strong character, my children can overcome these obstacles.

Trinette wants to be an actress or a doctor. Simon likes computers and hopes to focus on computer science and develop computer games. Martin would like to be a professional baseball player.

CASE ANALYSIS OF MIDDLE-CLASS BLACK FAMILIES

While the lot of middle-class black families is a significantly better one than that lived by poor and working-class black families, there are challenges that the members confront on a daily basis. These challenges are met with determination, a focus on how far African Americans have advanced in American society, and a recognition of how far they must continue to go.

Adequate access to health care and insurance helps middle-class families deal with medical concerns. Consequently, the Hart and Allen families reported no such problems in their respective case studies. Familiarity with effective interventions assists the children of middle-class families in reaching high levels of academic achievement, despite impediments such as learning disabilities. Sherry Hart, through her knowledge of educational methods, pushed to have two of her children tested. This resulted in diagnoses of an attention deficit disorder and a learning disability, respectively. Both children are successful in school thanks to timely interventions and modifications. In this way, Sherry Hart's professional experience and knowledge has the added benefit of empowering her to intervene and advocate for a positive educational experience for her children. This is an advantage that assists both of the children experiencing difficulty in school as well as her youngest daughter, who was invited to participate in a gifted program. Aware of the inadequacies of some gifted programs, the Harts declined to enroll their daughter.

The parents of the Hart and Allen families are all college-educated, likely encouraged by the achievement of their own parents—at least one parent of each spouse earned a baccalaureate degree. In the words of Peter Allen, education was "the key to getting out, to beating the system." For these families, education is armor to defend against the constant barrage of economic hardship and racism. Reginald Hart's social service administration degree, coupled with wife Sherry's education degree, provides a measure of security for the family as the degrees are in professions in which there is a constant need of well-trained workers. This is also true for the Allens—Peter holds a degree in dentistry and Beverly is an educator.

Keeping with our overarching observation that black families exhibit a pattern of shared power and status with the relationship, both wives in these middle-class families have comparable levels of education compared to their husbands. Both mothers are professionals in the field of education, one of the preferred professions of the black middle class. This professional knowledge has allowed both Beverly Allen and Sherry Hart to assist their children. When her youngest child was prohibited from starting school because of a late birthday, Sherry Hart homeschooled her, teaching the child how to read before she enrolled in kindergarten. Additionally, both women have chosen exemplary schools in which to enroll their children. Another benefit of the mother's vocation is the fact that the children are involved in sports and extracurricular activities that enrich their educational experiences.

Education is a value emphasized to the children of black middle-class families. In the Allen home, a picture of Peter III, Peter's eldest son from his previous marriage, hangs prominently with the son in full academic regalia. The importance that the family places on academic achievement is further exemplified when Peter Allen shares that Peter III's mother, although no longer living with the family, financially contributed to his education. Despite the dissolution of the marriage, both parents were able to come together to promote the academic progress of their son—a graduate of two of the most selective universities in the country. The Harts reported that their children are actively encouraged to pursue higher education, and even the décor of their home features regalia from the parents' affiliation in a service fraternity and sorority.

Black middle-class families promote a sense of accountability and obligation in their children. Though they disagree over whether their eldest son, Simon, should work during the school year, the Harts agree that their children should "develop a sense of ownership and responsibility." The children are assigned chores, and the parents hold the children accountable for doing them by making it an expectation that they will do them on weekend mornings. The same expectation exists in the Allen home. No explicit incentive, such as an allowance, exists in either household. The egalitarian nature of the African American family suggests that all members have a contribution to make to the common good of the family irrespective of rewards.

Both the Allens and Harts emphasize their satisfaction in the racial and ethnic composition of their respective neighborhoods. As professionals, they understand the importance of presenting their children with the opportunity to learn to communicate across different cultures, and they find that interracial classrooms and friendships are positive experiences for their children— not just interactions with whites, but with members of many ethnic groups. However, both families are proud of their ethnic background and feel that it is important to pass on the legacy to their children. The Harts have decorated their home with African American art, and the Allens celebrate Kwanzaa, an African American holiday.

There are some challenges for black middle-class families when they are in the untenable position of being one of a small number of African Americans in the community. Sherry Hart recounted an experience during which her son Martin was removed from his class during Black History Month for a history lesson. The boy's reaction was that there was a shameful aspect to the African American experience, as this information was not shared with his classmates. Sherry chose to react to this experience by engaging in a dialogue with the teacher and suggesting that black history was a topic that all students needed to learn about. Beverly Allen states that she wishes to raise children that are "truly colorblind, who have a distinct pride in their ethnicity." While black middle-class parents desire that their children be judged, and judge others by, in the words of Martin Luther King, Jr., "the content of their character," they also want their children to grow up with a sense of their proud cultural heritage.

Despite the successes that black middle-class families experience, the parents often feel a responsibility to prepare their children for the reality of an America that continues to discriminate against African Americans. Sherry

Hart feels it is her responsibility to educate her children and to help them develop a strong character, as armor to repudiate the "overt racism in our society." She also differentiates between the challenges that await her sons as black males and the sexism that her daughter will have to overcome. Beverly Hart is similarly concerned about the social status of black males and cites media influences as a problem in their portrayal. However, she sees the church as an ally in combating this negative imagery.

Organized religion plays a role in both families' lives, with the wives and children attending services on a regular basis. As evidenced by Beverly Hart's previous comment, the church offers more than spiritual guidance—it is also a bulwark against racism. While Peter Allen is not active in the church, he supports his wife's participation, as well as the children's attendance. Beverly Allen eschews official positions, but she acknowledges that she serves the church when asked. The Harts also cite involvement in the church as service. The involvement of black middle-class families in the church seems to center around a desire to serve others who have been less fortunate than they and to gain spiritual strength to deal with the challenges of life in America.

Similar to the poor and working-class families we have analyzed, middle-class black families exhibit egalitarian decision-making processes. The families often utilize a process in which one parent makes decisions on behalf of the family in some arenas, while the other parent makes decisions in others. For instance, the Harts moved often due to Reginald's military career. This made collaborative decision-making about their moves more or less impossible. However, after Reginald's retirement, the Harts agreed that whoever found employment first would determine where the family would move. It so happened that Sherry was hired first; therefore, the Harts moved to Arizona and Reginald found work soon after. Sherry also toured the neighborhoods and selected potential homes for the family, and Reginald and the children chose their house from this group. Such a method allowed for all members of the household to play a decision-making role. The Allens' search for a home went a little differently, as Beverly both toured the house and bid on it without consultation from Peter or the children; however, judging from the near decade the family has spent there, it seems that she was empowered to make a decision on behalf of the family.

There is a more concrete and shared responsibility among the parents, which is the responsibility of disciplining the children. Both the Allens and Harts feel that whichever parent is present should handle any discipline issues, as they feel consistency leads to well-behaved children. Since all of the children in both families are well behaved and have experienced few or no negative experiences with law enforcement, it can be argued that this approach is a successful one. Childrearing is of primary importance to both the Allen and Hart parents. They express concern over their children's television watching and the content of the music they listen to.

In summary, black middle-class families exhibit a drive and determination that has allowed them to participate fully in the social, political, and work realms in America. The climb to the summit of the American dream has been neither smooth nor easy for these families, but their work ethic and subscription to ideals, such as hard work and an abiding belief in the power of the Constitution, has produced positive effects for current and future generations.

4

Working-Class Black Families

THE BANKS FAMILY CASE STUDY

By Dorothy E. Dottin

Donald and Edna Banks are a black family with two children, Jake, fourteen, and Sheila, ten. Both parents are thirty-six years of age. The parents have been married for sixteen years. Both were born in Georgia and moved north after they married. They decided to start a family a few years later.

They reside in Providence, Rhode Island, in a two-family dwelling. They live on the first floor and Edna's mother and father occupy the second floor. They all seem very comfortable together.

Donald is head of the Banks household and Edna, the mother, returned to part-time work as soon as the children were in a full-day school program. Recently they arranged for the children to attend an after-school program from 3:00 to 5:00 P.M. For the after-school program, a van meets the children at school, takes them to the program, and brings them home after the program ends each evening. Edna is considering full-time employment in light of this recent "blessing" of after-school care for the children.

Both parents graduated from high school but could not afford to go on to college, although they now are considering part-time enrollment in college if possible financially.

All are members of a Baptist church they attend each week. Both parents are in the choir and one child is enrolled in Sunday school. The other child is not because she is autistic, but the church nursery extends babysitting care to her. Both children attend the neighborhood elementary school. Jake is in the fourth-grade advanced class, and Sheila is in a special-needs classroom for autistic students whose age group is eight to ten. Sheila has limited speech, is low-functioning developmentally delayed, and is emotionally disturbed. Sheila's autistic-like behaviors include spinning and running around in circles, staring at bright lights for indefinite periods, and staring into space for twenty-five to thirty seconds, which can be an indication of a kind of seizure activity.

Jake is able to follow directions well. Sheila, on the other hand, needs repeated cues for a response to occur. Developmentally, she is on the two-to-three-year age level somewhat similar to what is referred to as the "terrible twos," where most of the requests asked of her receive a negative response. Therefore, a firm behavior modification is applied so that some degree of discipline is achieved. The grandparents spoil their grandchildren, but not to the point of disrupting behavior modification applications. They do understand the necessity of it.

Jake may consider college if he chooses, will be encouraged to do so, but the choice will be his. Edna and Donald hope Sheila will achieve the appropriate skills necessary to maintain employment in a sheltered workshop setting where she will be able to earn a living so that she can establish some degree of independence.

The family is very close, including the grandparents, aunts, uncles, cousins, and other family members. They are polite to their neighbors, but do not visit them.

They live in a racially mixed neighborhood, in a very attractive setting. The homes are well kept and the streets are very clean.

Edna, Donald, and the children enjoy breakfast together as a family, and they have supper with the grandparents at least twice weekly. Donald, who is a construction laborer, has to be at work by 7:00 A.M. Since the family rises at 6:00 A.M., they have a light breakfast each morning. Donald leaves at 6:30 A.M., Edna showers, dresses, and gets the children ready so that when the school bus arrives, they are ready to board. Edna is a cashier at the neighborhood supermarket from 10:00 A.M. to 2:00 P.M., but she is considering extending her hours, as the extra money would come in handy.

The children return home by 5:30 P.M., and supper is finished by 6:30 P.M. Jake does his homework and Sheila is allowed to watch some TV. Both children retire by 9:00 P.M. Edna and Donald go to bed after the eleven o'clock news.

On Saturdays, they all sleep until 9:00 A.M., have breakfast, and do the family shopping. They have lunch out and usually return by 3:00 P.M. Edna does her wash and housework, and Donald does repair work around the house. The children visit the grandparents and dine together. Sometimes they go for a ride and ice cream or take in a PG-rated movie.

On Sundays, the family sleeps until 9:00 A.M., have breakfast, and go to church. They return home, have a light lunch, and the grandparents usually fix Sunday dinner, which is served around 4:30 P.M. The children remain with them and Edna and Donald take in a movie. They look forward to this time alone and the grandparents are more than willing to baby-sit. They realize that the parents need to spend quality time together because their life has been no bed of roses since the arrival of Sheila.

The family income is slightly above the federal poverty line; rent from the grandparents is used to supplement the family's income. All of the homes in their neighborhood are two-family, with two parents and two to three children in the households. The Bankses are nicely behaved and get along with one another comfortably. The parents agree that this is their last move.

Police availability is adequate, and the neighbors are satisfied with their present performance. Occasionally there is a need for police presence, but not very often. Drug activity was on the rise, but the troublesome family moved, minimizing the need for police.

The apartment has three bedrooms, a kitchen, a living room, one and a half baths, and a dining room. Both apartments are alike. The Bankses have one TV, a console in the living room. In addition, they have a stereo with speakers and a radio. The children have a good-sized record collection as Edna and Donald do. They enjoy music and often opt for it in lieu of TV.

All of the TV shows that the children watch are monitored and are age-appropriate. They have the newspaper delivered daily and on Sundays, and they subscribe to *Jet, Ebony, Time,* and *Newsweek.*

The Bankses have a telephone and use it to keep in touch with their friends and family here and out of state.

Donald helps Jake with his homework. Both parents and the grandparents teach the children manners, and all adults care for them when they are ailing. Edna and Donald assign chores for both children (minimal for Sheila). Both parents attend parent meetings; they usually agree on what candidates to vote for and what schools their children will attend. They jointly agree on furniture and car purchases and have agreed that they will have no more children.

Edna and Donald belong to two church and school organizations. The Bankses vacation with Edna's parents yearly while attending Donald's family reunion.

One of the happiest times of their lives was when they were finally able to purchase a home. The saddest time was when Sheila was diagnosed as autistic.

Donald and Edna felt that there was something amiss with their daughter, but they decided to wait until her entrance into nursery school. After a few weeks in that setting, the head teacher called them in, expressed her feelings about Sheila, and urged them to have her diagnostically evaluated. This conversation cemented the fears they had felt, but both parents felt that Sheila was put here by God and that her life must have some meaningful purpose.

After the confirmation, they gradually began to accept that Sheila would never be "normal" and that they must work with whatever skills Sheila had and could acquire in the future. It has been a difficult pill for them to swallow, but they are working hard to adjust slowly but surely; they are working it out. They are beginning to accept the fact that Sheila will be dependent on them, and, through counseling, she will learn ways to cope. They feel that they are lucky to have Edna's parents with them because they are very understanding and help them out every chance they get.

Both children are very much loved.

Summation

Autism is an emotional cross to bear in families. Many are able to cope quite well by making the best of what they have to work with, while others refuse to face up to the fact that such a problem exists.

The Bankses see their child's handicap as one of God's handiworks, and they believe that Sheila's life will have a purpose. Their strong faith in God is sustaining them and helping them to do the very best they can for both children. They accept Sheila as she is, work with whatever skills she is able to master, and help her to build up her self-confidence to do the very best job she is able to do.

THE TODD FAMILY CASE STUDY

By Shannon M. Stanton

The Todd family is working class. They live in Oakland, California. Currently, this family lives with the wife's parents. When this interview was conducted, Mrs. Todd was busy at work getting lunch ready for the children she watches in her day care business. She runs a day care center from her home, though at this time she cares for only three children. Her husband is a security guard for a local high school. Mrs. Todd (whose name is Darlene) smiles as she tells me that the students call her husband "Narc." "It's not that the students don't like him; they actually love him. However, it is his duty to catch the class cutters and the ditchers, and they don't understand why their 'homey' 'narcs' on them," said Darlene. Mr. Todd (whose name is Carl) coaches the boy's junior varsity basketball team. There are two children in the Todd family: Carl Junior (called Junior), age seven, and Theresa, age five.

Darlene met Carl during her last year in high school. He was working at a car dealership. Smiling, Darlene said, "When he saw me I knew he was whipped; from that point on, it was all history." They were married two years later, both were in their twenties, although Carl was six years older than his bride.

Darlene's parents have a six-bedroom house in which they have lived for the past thirty years. Now it is the residence for her parents, one of her sisters, and the Todd family. Darlene and her family of four occupy one large room that is fully equipped with a kitchenette. In this single room, there are two children's beds on one side, one with a *Lion King* comforter and the other with a *Beauty and the Beast* comforter. A queen-sized bed is in the corner of the room, a short distance from the twin beds. When I asked her if living together was hard, Darlene said it is hard for a whole family to live together in one room but God has blessed them with this living arrangement. This is their third time living at her mother's house, and she readily admits that she would like to move away for good. This current stay in Darlene's parents' home has been the longest—three years going on four—and the children are arriving at the age when they will need separate bedrooms. "When we first came to stay with my parents, Junior was four and Theresa two, but now with them seven and five, it becomes more complicated."

The Todd family moved in with Darlene's parents because of their financial condition. They never intended to stay as long as they did. However, complacency settled in and they became less aggressive in sticking with their goals. Darlene and Carl hold themselves responsible, because whenever they had any extra cash, they would spend it instead of saving it. They are now back on track with their plans to move out soon. The main issue of concern is "space," not only with bedrooms for the children, but they need personal space from the authority of Darlene's parents. Carl believes that their marital problems will get better when they move to their own place.

Darlene was employed as a parent counselor in a preschool program, but she quit when she decided that she was needed more at home. Theresa was about to start kindergarten, and their son, Junior, second grade. It was a family decision that Darlene was needed full-time at home. When Darlene was employed, she paid the rent and Carl paid for everything else, including two car notes, insurance, groceries, and other expenses. Darlene's check not only paid the rent, but she had to provide money for school clothes and household needs. Darlene said, "I prayed first, and just trusted God that it was the correct decision to stop working." Darlene had so much trust that she quit her job before she started her home day care business for other children; she knew in her heart that it was the right decision because in her hierarchy of values, the children come first.

The Todds definitely want their children to have more than they have; this is why Darlene pushes them in school. She pushes education more than her husband does; she said the children would be going to college, "no ifs, ands, or buts about it." Her husband is of the same mind, but he does not emphasize education as much as Darlene does. He actually tells her to stop pressuring them at such an early age. They are constantly butting heads when it comes to this issue. For example, Darlene felt Junior needed a math tutor. When she mentioned this fact to Carl, "he gave me reasons beginning from A to Z as to why Junior did not need one." Darlene plans not to say another word about a tutor until Junior receives his report card with an unsatisfactory grade in math. She is determined that her children receive the best education possible. Darlene is at school three to four times a week to see how well her kids are doing and to observe the teachers' instruction. Currently she is dissatisfied with both of her children's teachers. Darlene is trying to give her children the push in education that her parents were unable to give her.

Now that she is twenty-nine years old, Darlene realizes the importance of having an education and has decided to go back to school to obtain a B.A. degree. She will continue her day care business during the day and attend school at night. Darlene also is considering closing her childcare business and working part-time as an instructional aide instead, which would allow her to be home with the children, receive a steady income, and go to school.

The disciplining of the children falls mostly in Darlene's hands, though she states that "it's not by choice." Her husband plays the role of the children's friend to the point where "the children cannot distinguish when daddy is trying to exert authority or is just teasing." For example, Darlene said, "If Carl tells the children to stop doing something, he has to repeat himself five times before he gets any reaction, and half the time that reaction is the wrong one." Darlene can stop her kids with a particular tone of voice or a look that merely states, "you better stop what you're doing if you don't want your butt whipped." Darlene attributes the different ways of parenting that she and Carl exhibit to their upbringing. She was raised in a household where both her mother and father had that certain "look." Carl's father left home when Carl was young. As the oldest male child, however, a new responsibility fell on his shoulder; he was now the "man of the house." The living conditions of Carl's family were not great. His siblings were constantly in trouble, and all have a police record. Carl was the only child in his family who graduated from high school and did not have a police record. Straight from high school he went into military service, which Darlene believes was a blessing that saved him from "street mess."

Clearly Carl tries to give to his children everything he missed in his young life, but his style of rearing children conflicts with how Darlene wants to raise them. The children can ask their daddy for anything and Carl will do everything in his power to get what they ask for. He has no concept of "no" with them. Darlene is the sole disciplinarian who runs the household emotionally as well as spiritually. Carl is in charge of finances. "That is one thing with Carl, he does not mess around when it comes to paying the bills. That is why he is so adamant that I be able to provide the rent." Carl was previously married to a woman who absolutely destroyed his credit and he is not going to let that happen again.

Living with Darlene's parents does provide the Todd family with extra support. Theresa, the daughter, absolutely adores her grandmother; and her grandmother adores her. Oftentimes the two go shopping together and receive manicures. It was Darlene's mother who introduced Darlene and Carl to a strong spiritual faith. They started going to church together as a family. One thing that Darlene and Carl strongly agree on is that the children must be rooted in the teachings of Christ. For this family, their faith allows them to keep going when the times get rough.

The Todd family would like to move to a more racially diverse neighborhood. The home in which this extended family lives is the only black household in the neighborhood. The racial composition of the neighborhood today remains unchanged from her childhood years. Darlene wants more children in the neighborhood who look like her children.

The Todds do not travel or take vacations. However, Darlene believes that their children get a lot of knowledge about the world from school. Also, the children watch television programs that are monitored by Darlene and Carl. Most of the time, the children watch Christian videos or a Disney movie. "I don't want them picking up on all the slang and violence in the world," said Darlene. "They need to be kids."

Darlene is very close to her sisters. She calls them her support group. "They were all raised in the church, and now they seek to have Christ in every aspect of their lives." That is very important to Darlene. She said that she has drawn closer to the Lord over the past three years, and she knows Him to be a lifesaver for her soul and her marriage. Because of her religion, Darlene is not quick to temper, "especially when it comes to Carl. I just give it to Jesus and go on." Carl looks to his family of procreation as his support. Sometimes he doesn't understand Darlene's closeness with her sisters in her family of orientation. Darlene said, "He's learning. We just had two different lifestyles growing up; you couldn't tell me at twenty that would cause problems in the marriage, but now at twenty-nine, I definitely know better."

Though the problems seem both few and many, the parents in this family know they love each other and their children. And mostly, they believe that God is able to see them through any storm that comes their way.

CASE ANALYSIS OF WORKING-CLASS BLACK FAMILIES

Black working-class families live betwixt and between. Their income is above the federal poverty line but at or below the national mean. Most parents in these families have graduated from high school but few have a college degree. Husbands and fathers tend to have steady work in relatively difficult jobs that may place their lives at risk physically, such as that of construction laborer or security guard. These kinds of jobs bring in enough money to permit the wife and mother in the black working-class family to seek part-time employment if she chooses not to work full-time. More important, the steady income permits black working-class families to plan for the future.

While the family is the most important institution affecting the way of life of members of the black working-class, there is some reaching out to and participation in other agencies such as schools and churches.

Intact black working-class families tend to be stable because they follow customary ways of behaving. Marriage seldom occurs before the husband or wife is twenty years old; the number of children per family is relatively small (two or three); and, both families in this study had been married to the same mate for eight years or more.

The importance of family as a primary source of mutual assistance (especially for members down on their luck) is revealed in these case studies. Carl and Darlene Todd and their two children have had to return to the home of Darlene's parents three times to eke out a living when hard times were encountered. Darlene had a sister who also continued to live at home, after the Todd family moved in.

In the Banks family, the grandparents live in a house owned by their daughter and son-in-law, a pattern of living that is opposite to that for the Todd family that lives in a house owned by the grandparents. Regardless of who owns the property, these close encounters in one house by two families is for the purpose of rendering mutual assistance, even though the grandparents in the Banks family pay rent and have a separate floor in a two-family house owned by the younger generation.

The older and younger households that live near each other may dine together one or two times a week, and especially on Sundays. Grandparents are very good babysitters when parents in the younger generation go to a movie or some other form of entertainment alone. Because of the crowded condition of their situation of two families living in a single-family housing unit, Darlene and Carl Todd are troubled by the lack of privacy. While there are assets associated with extended families living together in the same housing unit, the absence of privacy is a liability for the black working class.

Black working-class families tend to live in densely populated urban areas. However, their interaction with neighbors is miniscule, in part because of their many family responsibilities, their frequent interaction with other relatives, and their long workday. These unique experiences of the black working class leave little time to fraternize with the members of other households in the neighborhood. One wonders, also, whether their limited involvement with neighbors is due to a lack of trust in strangers, so characteristic of the urban way of life.

There is evidence that working-class black families have an evolving understanding that they cannot go it alone. Because of this, they reach out and connect with the schools and churches. These are institutions and agencies they have learned to trust.

An example of this outreach is regular church attendance by both families in these case studies. Darlene and Carl Todd sing in the choir. Donald and Edna Banks belong to their church organizations. They call all opportunities that come their way "blessings." Darlene and Carl confess that their faith keeps them going when times are rough.

When Darlene Todd stopped working full-time to give attention to her children and the kind of education they were receiving in school, she prayed to God, hoping to receive some indication that this was the right thing to do. Religion seems to be an important source of support for the black working class.

The other community agency to which working-class families reach out is the school. Darlene Todd wants to do the right thing for her children with reference to education because of her desire for her children to have a better future than she and her husband could look forward to when they were children. Thus, she is determined to provide the best education possible for each of the Todd offspring, including college. She visits the public school two or three times a week to keep an eye on what is happening.

Edna and Donald Banks also want their son to attend college but will leave the decision up to him. Their daughter is autistic, a fact that they suspected but did not really know until informed by a schoolteacher. Through joint planning with the school, a protocol for the education of the mentally challenged daughter in the Banks family has been developed. By reaching out to and joining with school and church, black working-class families have found ways of containing the liability of disease, disability, and other hardships.

While some black working-class families may try to live on the paycheck of the husband alone, eventually they recognize the importance of a dual income to achieve their family values and aspirations. In the Banks and Todd families, fathers are employed full-time and mothers work full-time and part-time.

Joint contributions to family income seem to confer upon both parents joint power pertaining to family decision making. While the father was designated as head of household in the Banks family interview, family members also said that the father helps the children with their homework, both parents teach the children manners, and both care for the children when they are sick and assign chores to them when they are well. The husband and wife attend parent meetings at school. Decisions on how to vote, what schools children will attend, what furniture to buy, what health care to purchase, and how many children to have are joint decisions. Even if the father is designated as the head of the household, the decision-making power of this role is shared. It is appropriate to classify the Banks family as egalitarian.

While the wife seems to be the more powerful person in the Todd family in that she visits school often to protect the children's interests and is the chief disciplinarian, she and her husband are constantly "butting heads" about money matters, such as retaining a tutor in mathematics for their son. The father also tries to prevail upon his wife not to put so much pressure on the children to succeed in school. In this regard, the father is the advocate for the children in family councils. Both parents acknowledge that the husband in the Todd family is in charge of finances. Yet, he was adamant in encouraging his wife to take a job that would enable her to pay the rent. While the Todd family is experiencing conflict over whose family life ideal should prevail, neither the father nor the mother is fully in control of all matters. Thus, it is fair to classify the Banks family as tending toward egalitarianism, while it now drifts between both matriarchal and patriarchal dominance. Thus far, the husband and wife do not seem to possess the negotiating skills needed to fulfill the requirements of egalitarianism toward which the decision-making structure of their family is tending.

The limited income of black working-class families and their high aspirations leaves little time for vacations and other recreational activities. Beyond involvement with the church and the school, black working-class families have little, if any, involvement in other community associations.

Parents work hard and long in black working-class families to provide opportunities for their children that eluded them during childhood. To fulfill this mission, black working-class families tend to link up with extended family members for mutual assistance before turning to others for help, although there is increasing evidence that these families have a reasonable amount of trust in schools and churches.

5

Low-Income Black Families

THE ROBY FAMILY CASE STUDY

By Matthew Ryan

Born in Florida, the eldest of two children of a noncommissioned Navy officer, Diane Roby has lived in six states prior to settling in her present neighborhood, a low-income tenement section of Springfield, Massachusetts. Today, in her late twenties, this intelligent woman finds herself the unemployed mother of two children, refusing public assistance, and dependent on sporadic child support payments from the children's father, unemployment compensation, and the financial assistance of her younger sister with whom the apartment is shared.

Ms. Roby's children, Maralyn, age seven, and Malcolm, age four, are both healthy and active. On the day of the interview she is resting some strained muscles acquired as the result of an auto accident two days earlier. Her old Pontiac sits parked in the street, threatening to make Ms. Roby a permanent pedestrian. Maralyn is at school, and, during the interview, Malcolm amuses himself by manipulating the television remote and removing items from the kitchen for deposit on the living room carpet. The three-bedroom apartment is old but well kept and Ms. Roby, with a tone of resignation, comments on the perpetual effort needed to keep it reasonably clean while caring for the children. "My life is boring, I'm getting lazy and I have no self-esteem. I eat, watch TV soaps, and take care of the kids. . . . It's the same every day, I need something else."

While as a teen Ms. Roby had no specific goal, neither did she expect her life to be what it has become. Her childhood was a series of Navy bases and adolescence brought the demands of "churchgoing," choir, and ROTC. In her junior year of high school, her family transferred to Massachusetts. Discovering her high school pregnancy, six months prior to graduation, her father, with the family's support, "forced" her to have an abortion so that she could continue her schooling. On graduation day she handed her father her diploma, refused his offer to assist her entry into college, found a job as an assembler at a computer company, and began her life as an adult. A year later she met Dwight, the father of her two children. Although they never married, their relationship lasted five years. She admits that the relationship was "never good" and that it ended on the day she returned home from the hospital with their youngest child and found another woman in her house. Now, three years later, Dwight and the other woman still live together only several houses away.

Her life as a single parent has been difficult. The separation with Dwight sent Diane into a deep depression and an attempt at suicide requiring a month's hospitalization. During this time, her sister, with the help of neighbors and friends, cared for the children. They were later sent to their grandparents in Kentucky for several additional weeks. Within six months, Ms. Roby returned to her work as an assembler with a new company, a low-paying job she found boring but kept because she liked "the people and the pace." When business slowed a few months ago, she was let go and has been unemployed since. She would like to find another job, "Anything that gets me out of the house," she relates, "I'm not going to be picky." Her medical insurance runs out this month and just talking about trying to get by without coverage brings tears to Ms. Roby's eyes. Increasingly, her limited resources force her to visit church pantries for food and thrift stores for clothing. The threat of being unable to pay her rent troubles her often.

Presently, Ms. Roby continues to resist government assistance beyond a small amount of monthly food stamps. Her tone turns angry while discussing her dealings with the staff at the welfare office. "There are people in this city going without help. . . . The [welfare] workers are not trying to help, they look down on you. . . . They're assholes."

She has been unsuccessful in her attempt to find day care for Malcolm. During the last few months of her employment, she was paying a substantial amount of her weekly income for childcare. "I was only working to pay the childcare center," she related and continued, saying that she needed a sliding scale program but none was available. "I was poor when I was working; I'm even poorer now," she concluded.

The rent on the family apartment is more than what she receives in unemployment benefits and periodic child support from Dwight, who works for the local electric company. She is nearing the end of her monthly receipt of unemployment benefits. Her sister pays one-third of each month's rent from her low-paying job as a receptionist. Even with her sister's assistance,

Ms. Roby fears that unless her depression is stabilized and she finds employment, she may soon need to move again, this time near her parents in Kentucky. If so, this would be her fourth apartment in three years. Although she would like a yard for the children, she would prefer to remain where she presently lives. She described the neighborhood as poor and racially mixed. She notes the presence of many college students in the area despite its relatively high level of crime and drug activity. She reports that her neighbors mostly keep to themselves, so friends are difficult to acquire. "I have a few friends, but mostly associates," she observes. She reports only being involved in one serious racial incident in her lifetime. This involved being slapped and pushed by other black girls while in high school because of her light brown skin and long, straight hair.

The children are very important to Ms. Roby and she expresses high expectations for their future. She insists that they will both graduate from high school: "They will grant me that, just as I honored my father." Beyond this, she hopes that they will also complete college as her younger sister, with whom they live, has done. Each month she plans a few "fun suppers," allowing the children to pick the food and follow dinner with a game or video. Usually, eating together is reserved for these special occasions. The children's high activity level results in frequent reprimands, she confesses. She hears herself echoing admonishment once used by her mother, although she is quick to respond to being close to them. "I live for my kids," she insists.

Each year she makes a trip to Kentucky for a family visit, usually on the Fourth of July. During the remainder of the year, she receives a phone call from her parents each Sunday. On her last monthly visit to Kentucky, she joined together with her many cousins and helped build her grandparents a house on their small farm. Until then, they lived in a home without indoor plumbing, although through the years fifteen children were raised under its roof. She takes pride in recalling that five generations were present when her grandfolks moved into the home built for them.

Although Ms. Roby admits watching hours of "soaps" each day on TV, her main leisure activity is dancing on Sunday nights at a downtown club. "I love dancing," she remarked with excitement. At the club, she also makes extra money "lip-syncing" to the music on stage. Other evenings her sister or another "associate" watches the children as she visits with a male friend that she has recently started dating.

Two events stand out as the happiest times of her life: the birth of her first child and her graduation from high school, despite the circumstances. The low point of her life is the regret and sadness she still feels for not being present when her grandmother died several months ago. "She was always there for me when I wanted to talk," she reminisced through fresh tears.

Ms. Roby views her future with the hope that her children will be successful. She is somewhat less optimistic about her own future, as if to protect against repeated disappointment. "People say I'm too kind, too naïve, . . . too trusting. I often get used, so I know I should stick more to myself. But I know I'm going to come upon a person who really needs my help . . . and I want to be there to help that person."

Ms. Roby has hope, but the future will not be easy to master in Massachusetts. Her repeated periods of depression, the lack of low-cost childcare, the state's high unemployment rate, racial discrimination, and her present financial debt may force her to return to Kentucky. For the truly poor, the road out of poverty is mired with obstacles.

THE MARSH FAMILY CASE STUDY

By Elisabeth Maia Kling

George Marsh grew up in a poor black home in the heart of Detroit. The fourth child in a family of seven, George was his mother's only legitimate child. His father was an alcoholic who spent most of his time away from home, in bars, and on the streets. Mrs. Marsh, as George recalls, was the one who held the family together. Like her children, she was afraid of her husband. As George puts it, "She was always ducking him." However, "she always cared for us kids." On three separate occasions George was beaten unconscious by his father, who often came home drunk. Mrs. Marsh took George to the hospital and eventually filed suit in the courts for child abuse. She and her mother were both very religious women, and George remembers that they always prayed for him and said that the Lord was going to save him. As children, George and his brothers and sisters always went to church. Religion was a major part of their lives.

George revealed, however, that by the age of thirteen, he seemed to be following in his father's footsteps. He had begun drinking, had become violent, and was prone to emotional outbursts. By the age of fifteen, he had experienced severe problems in school and underwent psychiatric treatment for the first time. At sixteen, events took a brief turn for the better. George participated in a summer Upward Bound program for exceptional high school students. As George related this part of his story, a smile came to his face and a wistful look entered his eye. He remembered it fondly and said that this was one time in his life when he had really liked learning. George and his Upward Bound instructors knew that he "wasn't dumb," and they were "open." This was also where he met Lillian.

Returning to the city and the high school routine after his summer on the suburban college campus was difficult for George. He felt frustrated. He began to drink again, he used drugs, and he ran around with a gang. By this time he was an alcoholic, and he confessed, "I drank a lot, a whole lot."

Meanwhile, George and Lillian started spending more and more together. She was fifteen years old, a high school sophomore, and he, at seventeen, was a junior. Her parents did not approve of George, but she loved him. In the spring of that year they both dropped out of school and started living together.

A year passed and George's involvement with the street and his gang continued. His employment at odd jobs was sporadic. Lillian had, by then, given birth to their first child. She and the new baby depended on welfare for support. Her family continued to demonstrate hostility toward George and urged Lillian to return home with the baby. Lillian chose to stay.

George knew that things were not going well. Speaking of this time, he said that he realized he loved Lillian and the baby but that he "couldn't get it together" in his head. He felt like running away and leaving them because he was afraid he could not be a good father. When Lillian got pregnant for the second time, George left and joined the army.

He did not make it through boot camp. The discipline was too rigid and the life too strict. The army put him to work as a dishwasher in the base hospital. At home, Lillian continued to care for the family and remained faithful to George. Her support proved invaluable to him. However, his mental problems persisted, and he wound up in the psychiatric ward of the base hospital. George said, "I knew I had some serious things going on in my head, but I didn't know how to fix them up." A few months later he was discharged from the service.

After his discharge, George went home to Lillian, and his old life resumed. He returned to drinking, took up drugs, became violent, became involved with other women, and had several encounters with the law. Of this period, he said, "I did it all." At the same time, though, he began to provide more regularly for Lillian and the four children. He and a friend embarked on a business venture together and wrote "jingles" for television and radio. George liked it because it was creative, expressive, and original. For the first time in a long time, he felt good.

The good feelings did not last, however. One day, his "business partner" abruptly decided to leave town. George's father, then in Arkansas, died; his mother, in Detroit, died several months later. Shortly thereafter, a niece, who had been living with him and Lillian, also died. Life seemed to crumble, and Lillian was pregnant for the fifth time. George checked into the local psychiatric hospital as a "day patient."

During this time Lillian continued to care for the children during the day and was home to talk with George when he returned from the hospital at night. George spoke of these as "hard times." Motioning to his needle-marked, worn arms, he showed me the spot on this wrist where he had already tried to kill himself twice. He also spoke of a third unsuccessful attempt using pills. The doctors, he said, had classified him as manic-depressive and

psychologically unstable. They told him that it would take him years to re-
cover. "But," he said, "Lillian was there through it all."

As a child, religion had played a major part in Lillian's life. She left the
church only when she met George and started living with him in high school.
Now, alone and in need, she turned to the City Mission Society and became
deeply involved in their worship services and children's programs. One day,
just after George's most recent suicide attempt, the City Mission Society
chaplain came to visit him at the hospital. George referred to this event as the
major turning point in his life. He said: "For the first time, I heard and understood the Gospel of Jesus Christ. This preacher wasn't talkin' the same
hell fire and brimstone that I had heard as a kid. He told me about the love
of God and the grace of God. Jesus offered me forgiveness and a new start."
George didn't imply that life immediately became easier after that. He did not
go into detail, but it became apparent that the process of rebuilding his life
had been slow, painful, and often frustrating. He told me about his brother,
who had once "got saved," but it happened too fast and did not last. For
George, it was slow but real.

Shortly after leaving the hospital, George became the caretaker of the
grounds at the City Mission Society, and Lillian worked there as a clerk. In
addition, George headed up the neighborhood City Mission Society athletic
program and worked with young boys. Together the family attended church
and participated in the weekday meetings and children's activities.

George cited this time as the period of greatest change in his life. Unlike
the earlier George, who had abused his children, had been unfaithful to his
wife, and had participated in violence, drugs, and crime, the new George
was working on learning to be a good father and providing for his family.
The move from their former apartment in a housing project to the apartment
in the Mission headquarters was a good one. They were still poor, but they
were able to make ends meet.

Today George and Lillian are the parents of five children: Renee, who is
fourteen and in the eighth grade; Curtis, who is thirteen and in the seventh
grade; Luther, who is twelve and in the sixth grade; Cedric, who is eleven
and in the fifth grade; and Linda, who is nine and in the third grade. In
three months they are expecting their sixth child. The entire family is ex-
cited.

Last year, George and Lillian decided to get married. They now live in a
rented apartment in a "fairly safe" neighborhood in Detroit. Although I did
not visit their home, it was obvious from George's description that his family
is, next to God, the most important part of his life. He said that they were trying to make things work, were "doing things together," and that "God gets
all the credit and glory." For fun, the family likes to go to the park or to the
movies. However, most of their time is taken up with work and school, and
visits to the park usually wait until special Saturdays.

When asked who makes the decisions in the family, George said, "We make them together." The family works as a team. He and Lillian feel that the children should be allowed to participate actively in the decision-making process of the family since they are a part of it, and "we won't always be there to help them. They need to learn now." George went on to explain that he thinks the world is a dangerous place and that he should know. He does not want his children to follow in his footsteps, but he does not want them to be afraid of the world either. He wants to expose them to it and teach them how to deal with it.

Lillian and George have an egalitarian marriage. They stated that now they both share the responsibilities of teaching the children manners, doing the cooking, assigning chores, deciding what church to attend, and dealing with other domestic issues. Lillian is more likely to care for the children when they are sick—though they rarely are—and to visit the children's teachers at school. She also decides what to prepare for meals and helps the children decide what to wear. George, on the other hand, made the decision to move out of the City Mission headquarters and into their present apartment.

Generally, the children get along well with one another. School is an important part of their lives, and, as George puts it, each one "takes to it" in a different way. Renee, like her father, has a creative streak and wants to be an artist. She hopes to go to college. Curtis, on the other hand, is not really interested in school. He works well with his hands and likes things having to do with space and astronauts. The family has had some problems with him in school. Luther, like his father, is an excellent athlete, and he likes science and math. He wants to work with computers. Cedric is the student of the family, and often his parents have to coax him from his books in order to "go outside and play some." George says that Cedric is the one who is most anxious to do things right and is very eager to please authority. Finally, Linda particularly enjoys reading and spelling bees. All of the children help one another with their homework, which is done around the kitchen table. George added that now that the children are growing up and becoming teenagers, peer pressure on them is greater. He, Renee, and Lillian have "had to talk a lot."

George and Lillian support their children and encourage them in whatever way they can. When asked what goals he and Lillian had for the children, George said that was their decision. He approves of Renee's desire to go to college, but he does not want to push her. He is not sure what it would take for Luther to be able to work with computers.

Neither George nor Lillian is active in politics. Sometimes, "if it matters," they vote. They get the news from watching television and listening to the radio.

Religion is the focal point around which all of life centers in the Marsh family. George feels that "God saved me for a reason." He believes he has received a calling to the ministry, which he considers a full-time commitment. To this end, he and Lillian set out to develop a "street ministry" after they left the City Mission Society headquarters. They receive help and support from the neighborhood Gospel Center, and their work is entirely supported by donations. George admits that finances are almost always "tight," but he does not classify himself or his family as poor. He and Lillian feel blessed.

CASE ANALYSIS OF LOW-INCOME BLACK FAMILIES

Living the life of a low-income black family is hard work, not a happy-go-lucky, carefree existence as imagined by some members of society who are not poor, and as portrayed sometimes in the movies.

First, the encounter with death is frequent among poor black people. Their death rate is probably higher than the death rate in any other population group in the United States, especially deaths from homicide and certain conditions originating in the perinatal period. At birth the life expectancy rate for black women and black men lags five to seven years behind the life expectancy of white women and white men. And illness, physical as well as mental, is exceedingly high in poor black families.

In the Marsh and Roby case studies of poor black families, the husband in the Marsh family, George, during his early twenties, lost his father and mother to death in a single year; shortly thereafter, a niece who had lived with the Marsh family died. George attempted suicide once or twice.

So unsettling were these losses and the demons he confronted in his mental illness that George checked himself into a psychiatric hospital as a day patient. He had been sick for a long time but did not know it until he was diagnosed as manic-depressive. Additionally, he was an alcoholic and used drugs.

While the wife and mother in the Marsh family was strong and steady, the mother in the Roby family was not. Diane Roby went into a deep depression after the loss of her husband by way of legal separation. Her depression was so severe that she attempted suicide, was unsuccessful, but required a month's hospitalization. She confesses that her life is boring and that she has no self-esteem.

The linkage of poor black family members to institutional systems that support and sustain other population groups is tenuous, fragile, and easily broken.

Employment has not been a continuous experience in either of these low-income families. Diane Roby worked in two semi skilled jobs as an assembler but was laid off from her last job when business slowed down. Now she is about to run out of her unemployment insurance. Her medical insurance, a fringe benefit of her last job, will end soon also.

George Marsh joined the army as a source of employment but couldn't make it through boot camp. Finally, George was offered a job as groundskeeper at the City Mission Society that also made available housing for his family. Now George wants to be a good father and a better provider for his family. George decided to move his family away from the City Mission Society as he and his wife, Lillian, were about to launch a "street ministry" as their joint vocation.

What one clearly sees in both low-income families in this study is the absence of continuity in almost all undertakings, including mates, employment, and housing. Diane Roby, for example, is having difficulty paying rent since losing her last job and is thinking of moving again, this time back to Kentucky to be near her parents.

The one constant experience that these low-income black families can count on is help from members of their family of orientation. They are present when needed to rescue the perishing. For example, Diane Roby's sister lives with her and her two daughters and pays one-third of the house rent. Diane also receives long-distance telephone calls once a week from her parents and is thinking about moving to be nearer to them. When hospitalized for depression, Diane sent her children to live with their grandparents.

The negative aspect of the helping hand always extended by parents, siblings, and relatives to members of low-income black families is that the extended hand sometimes may be classified as interference. The interference in the affairs of Diane Roby began during her senior year in high school when her father insisted that she have an abortion against her will so that she could finish her secondary education. That interference stimulated a rebellious attitude in Diane that she has only recently started to overcome. And the parents of Lillian Marsh did not approve of George when the couple dropped out of high school and started living together. Even after the first child was born, Lillian's parents still did not accept George and urged her to return home with the baby. Despite these occasional interferences, the family of orientation, into which each partner of the family of procreation was born, is always there to lend a helping hand in whatever way it can; frequently, it is the institution of last resort and sometimes the only institution that is willing to give continuous assistance to poor black family members.

As we see, in these two case studies, usually it is the daughter of a mother in the new family of procreation who has to resolve conflicts, if any, between her parents and her husband. With reference to family affairs in her new family, mothers continue to be the chief negotiator and sometimes the chief protector. George Marsh said that his mother always cared for the kids, and he gives credit to his wife for holding their family together. As a single mom after separating from her husband, Diane Roby tells everyone that the children are "very important" to her.

Decision making in the two-parent low-income household in this study is described by George Marsh, the father, as a team effort in which husband, wife, and children have a say in what will be done. It is true that the parents have different assignments (for example, the mother takes the lead role in caring for sick children and advising the children on what to wear, and the father decides where the family will live). However, other responsibilities (such as teaching the children manners, cooking, and deciding what church to attend) are shared. No one is the head of the household. Even the new "street ministry" that the Marsh family is launching is a family affair, with the husband and wife teaming up as partners in this enterprise. It, then, is appropriate to call this low-income black family an egalitarian family, despite the steady, strong, and stabilizing influence of the mother. It is not a matriarchal family structure.

The low-income status of black families in this study is largely due to the limited education of the parents, most of whom received less than a high school education and, therefore, have to take unskilled jobs that do not pay well.

Beyond these three factors mentioned above, a major problem that low-income families confront is the absence of continuity in much of what they do. There is an absence of continuity in employment, residential living, health status, and marriage partners. These stop-and-go experiences discourage or render impossible long-range household planning. It, therefore, is unfair to classify these families as hedonistic and unwilling to delay gratification. There is precious little in the low-income, black family experience that would gratify anyone. The major problem is that they have few, if any, institutional safety nets that offer sustained support and protection from the troubles of this world. About the only institutional system that seems not to have abandoned low-income black families is religion. Clearly, the City Mission Society and other churches with which Lillian Marsh has been affiliated taught her how to suffer the redemption of her husband from his wayward habits and helped her to develop the love and empathetic understanding in order to accept her husband as he was before trying to change him.

Moreover, the church provided a job and a place for the Marsh family to stay while getting back on their feet. And Diane Roby, who is having some severe financial problems, has found church pantries that give out food and thrift shops with low-priced clothing, a friendly and much-needed source of support. It is understandable why a good number of low-income black families hold tenaciously to their religion. So much is stacked up against them; yet they manage somehow to survive through prayer and supplication.

6

Alternative Family Forms

Benjamin Elijah Mays, spiritual mentor of Martin Luther King Jr. and former president of Morehouse College in Atlanta—which Charles Willie attended as a student decades ago—died in March 1984. This magnificent man left a unique legacy for educators, his educational philosophy of transcendency. Mays told his students: "You are what you aspire to be and not what you are now. . . . The tragedy of life doesn't lie in not reaching your goal. The tragedy lies in having no goal to reach" (Mays 1963: 1, 3).

Mays' attitude was characterized in a eulogy by one of his students, Samuel Cook, former president of Dillard University. Cook said of his mentor, "He had a divine romance with the world of higher possibilities" (31 March 1984). We give you a few examples of what happens when several different flowers are permitted to bloom and when we explore "higher possibilities" and alternative routes to excellence. The results of a study, *Five Black Scholars*, are instructive (Willie 1984).

John Hope Franklin, emeritus professor of the University of Chicago and Duke University, is a specialist in southern history. He was born in Oklahoma, attended Fisk University, graduated magna cum laude, and enrolled in Harvard where he earned a Ph.D. degree and forty years later was awarded an honorary doctoral degree. A founding member of the Phi Beta Kappa chapter at Fisk, Franklin eventually served as president of the Southern Historical Association, the American Historical Association, and the United Chapters of Phi Beta Kappa.

Franklin had a head start. His mother had a college education and was a teacher. He played on the back bench of her classroom when he was preschool age and learned to read at an early age by listening to the lessons his mother prepared for others. His father, also college educated, studied and practiced law. Franklin grew up in a family of professionals who urged him and his siblings to get an education; all of the children finished college following in the footsteps of their parents. John Hope Franklin was named in honor of the first black president of Morehouse College, a school his father attended.

Surrounded by learned parents who provided a strong support system, Franklin experienced achievements that were predictable outcomes of such an intellectually stimulating household. John Hope Franklin has been identified as the preeminent black historian in the United States in a study of five black scholars who were past-presidents of national professional associations (Willie: 1986 13–26).

In that same study, Kenneth B. Clark was voted one of the most renowned black psychologists in the nation. But his path to excellence was quite different from that of Franklin. Clark was born in the Panama Canal Zone of parents who migrated from Jamaica. When the marriage of his parents dissolved, he moved with his mother and his younger sister to New York City at the age of four. His mother worked in the garment industry and attended night school, eventually receiving a diploma. She was very supportive of Clark and urged him and his sister to go to college. She cared for the family as well as she could, imprisoned in a big-city ghetto where there were very few material rewards.

Clark graduated from Howard University and received a Ph.D. degree in psychology from Columbia University. For a third of a century, Clark taught at City College of New York. He retired as a distinguished university professor emeritus.

A member of Phi Beta Kappa and Sigma Xi, Clark headed national professional associations in his discipline, including the American Psychological Association and the Society for the Psychological Study of Social Issues. In addition, Clark served for several years as an elected member of the powerful New York State Board of Regents. He, also, was awarded an honorary doctoral degree by Harvard University.

There are similarities in the achievements of Franklin and Clark but gross differences in their backgrounds and pathways to excellence. Franklin came from a two-parent, middle-class family in which both parents were professionals. Clark grew up in a single-parent, working-class household in which his mother was the sole source of support. Working during the day and going to school at night, Clark's mother obviously could not provide constant supervision over a family whose children were coming of age in a big-city ghetto.

Other differences between the two men have to do with their geographic origins and social experiences. Franklin was southern born and southern reared while Clark was foreign born and northern reared. The risks, opportunities, dangers, and difficulties to which both scholars were exposed,

Franklin in Oklahoma and Clark in New York, when they were growing up were quite different as was their socioeconomic status. But these different circumstances and conditions seemed not to have made a difference in their achievements and reputations. They followed different paths to honor and glory. Yet each man succeeded in his endeavors, and both became accomplished scholars. The Franklin and Clark stories indicate that place of birth, family composition, socioeconomic status, education, occupation of parents, and region of residence may facilitate the achievement of excellence or serve as an impediment; but even as impediments, they can be transcended. There are different paths to honor and glory as revealed in the lives of these great men.

More disparate than the lifestyles of Franklin and Clark were the experiences of Matthew Holden Jr. and Darwin T. Turner. Holden is a political scientist who occupies an endowed professorship at the University of Virginia in Charlottesville. Turner, now deceased, was a specialist in literature and a distinguished professor at the University of Iowa. Both scholars were in their fifties when this study was conducted and had made significant contributions to the literature in their fields and to the professional associations of their disciplines.

Holden has been an elected member of the governing council of the American Political Science Association and has served as its vice president and president. In addition, he has been a board member of the Social Science Research Council and was appointed to the Assembly of Behavioral and Social Sciences of the National Academy of Science. Holden is also a public administrator, serving in the past as commissioner of the Wisconsin Public Service Commission and in a similar capacity with the Federal Energy Regulatory Commission in Washington, D.C. He has been a faculty member at approximately five different schools.

Turner has been a member of the board of directors of the Modern Language Association and the National Council of Teachers of English. In addition, he was a trustee of the National Humanities Center. Turner also was an educational administrator and served not only as department chair several times, but also as an academic dean. He has been a professor or administrator at approximately six different schools.

Matthew Holden Jr. was voted as one of the most outstanding black political scientists in the nation, and Darwin Turner, one of the most outstanding blacks specializing in literature. Beyond these striking similarities in career accomplishments at the mid-century mark in their lives, Holden's and Turner's pathways to honor and glory were radically different. The members of Holden's family were Mississippi farmers before joining the World War II migration of blacks to the city in search of jobs in industry. Turner came from a family of gifted intellectuals and professionals. His paternal grandfather was a college teacher and a public school principal, as was

Turner's maternal grandmother. His parents graduated from college, as did some of his grandparents. His mother received a master's degree in education, and his father studied pharmacy. Both pursued professions connected with their college training.

Members of Turner's family earned bachelor's and master's degrees, and his paternal grandfather, whom Turner described as a great inspiration, was a Ph.D. graduate in biology form the University of Chicago, the school from which Turner also received his terminal academic degree. His maternal great-grandfather was one of the first black teachers in Cincinnati. Thus education as a course of study and as a profession was part of the socialization experience of Turner. In this respect, his life was very different from that of Holden, whose parents were blue-collar workers on the farm and in the city.

Turner had a large, extended family in the city, as did Holden on the farm. There the similarity of their family experiences ended. Following crop failures, Holden's parents moved to Chicago to labor as unskilled workers. After finishing his studies in pharmacy, Turner's father moved to Chicago to establish three drugstores. His father commuted between Chicago and Cincinnati periodically, and his mother visited Chicago often. The burden of city life was too much for Holden's parents, both of whom had less than a high school education. Eventually they went separate ways. Holden remained in his mother's household where, he said, there was bread enough to eat but none to spare.

Turner whizzed through school, completing college summa cum laude in three years, earning a master's degree at the University of Cincinnati two years later, and earning a Phi Beta Kappa key—all by the age of eighteen. Holden's baccalaureate degree was acquired in a stop-and-go fashion: He spent four years at the University of Chicago, a time he described as a great experience and also one that overwhelmed him. He failed to complete his B.A. degree there but finished the degree two years later at Roosevelt University, also in Chicago. Holden earned a master's degree by the age of twenty-three. However, his stint in the armed forces and his jobs with county and metropolitan planning or charter commissions delayed further study for a while, and he did not complete his Ph.D. degree at Northwestern University until age twenty-nine. During these years, Holden was single and on his own. Turner also interrupted his studies for a Ph.D. degree—he taught in two colleges—but still received the degree by the age of twenty-five. He lived in Chicago with his wife and children, and he was also a student in the same city where his father owned a business. While Turner was on his own, he knew that a parent was near and could be turned to in times of trouble.

Despite differences in region of birth, childhood socialization experiences, education and occupation of parents, family composition, and personal educational progress, Holden and Turner came out on top with similar professional reputations. Both divided their careers between scholarship and administration. Both were high achievers in their respective disciplines and are examples of the multiple routes to success.

In summary, these outstanding black scholars in four fields grew up in a variety of family forms, including nuclear families and extended families, two-parent and single-parent households. The occupations of their parents ranged from unskilled and semiskilled workers to professionals and self-employed business managers. Some parents failed to finish high school; others finished college and attained graduate degrees. These black families could be classified as farm folk and cosmopolitan city dwellers. They had northern and southern roots.

These outstanding scholars had other varied experiences. One completed college in three years, two in four years, and one in six years. Two graduated from predominantly black colleges; two graduated from predominantly white colleges. One married before he was twenty; one married after he was thirty; two married at ages between these extremes. Two have taught in black and in white schools; two have taught extensively in predominantly white schools. There are different roads to excellence, as the lives of these scholars reveal.

We creatures of humanity have what Michael Murphy calls a "fuller reality" (Murphy 1969: 18). We have the capacity to transcend the concrete and the particular. We are people with purpose. Where there is purpose, there is choice. Where there is choice, there is freedom, and freedom is the basis of our many possibilities—those that are higher and those that are lower. We need to conform, to be rational and lawful. Without these attributes, there is chaos. But we also need to be free, creative, and spontaneous. Without these characteristics, there is atrophy and decay.

These four case studies of Professors Franklin, Clark, Holden, and Turner demonstrate the presence of purpose in the attitudes and actions of human beings. One purpose manifested in the lives of each of these persons was the attainment of excellence in his respective field of study. And, of course, all four chose to pursue excellence by traveling several different routes.

The case study method is particularly appropriate for helping us to understand the various ways that individuals may fulfill a common desire. We suppose that this fact was what Harvey Cox was thinking about when he said, "innovation . . . requires a variety of experiments going on, 'a hundred flowers blooming'" (Cox 1969: 59). All four scholars in our study were admirable and esteemed by their peers, despite their different ways of achieving excellence.

These case studies show that several factors mentioned in professional literature as impediments to academic achievement, such as low socioeconomic status and socialization in single-parent or fractured families, can

be and have been transcended. Specific examples are the achievements of
Kenneth Clark and Matthew Holden. They grew into adulthood living in
working-class, single-parent households. Nevertheless, the scholarship of
these individuals has been recognized and validated by the top professional
associations in their respective disciplines—the American Psychological Association of which Clark was elected president, and the American Political
Science Association of which Holden was elected president.

There is no evidence that the way of life in adulthood of these four outstanding scholars could be classified as "outside . . . American life" or living
in "a world of make-believe," labels E. Franklin Frazier attached to affluent
black families in his book, *Black Bourgeoisie* (1957).

What each of these scholars has accomplished has been central to the
American way of life. This is particularly true of Kenneth Clark and John
Hope Franklin who worked as researchers and expert witnesses with
lawyers of the plaintiff class in the *Brown v. Board of Education* court case
(1954) that ordered desegregation of public school education in the United
States. As indicated above, Matthew Holden served as commissioner of the
Wisconsin Public Service Commission and in a similar capacity with the Federal Energy Regulatory Commission. Holden's work with these state and federal agencies was central to the welfare of all.

Also, there is no evidence in the lives of these four scholars to support the
"oppositional culture hypothesis" set forth by John Ogbu. This hypothesis
asserts that low-income African American students, because of employment
discrimination, have developed a culture that denigrates achievement as
"acting white" (Fordham and Ogbu 1986). Clearly, these four scholars had a
positive attitude toward school and succeeded in their vocations as black
men. More will be reported on the source of their positive attitudes in chapter 7.

In a 1996 study, George Farkas discovered that African American students are more positive toward school than are whites (Farkas, 1996). Yet,
he and his associates declared, "it is premature to reject oppositional culture as one of the possible mechanisms influencing lower school performance among ethnic minorities and low-income students" (Farkas, Llevas,
and Maczuga, 2002: 153–154). Our findings regarding the educational
progress of these four scholars during childhood and adulthood are reasons for casting doubt on the validity of the oppositional culture hypothesis. Indeed, our study of alternative routes to excellence should encourage
more creative studies on how and why black students affiliated with low-
income families succeed.

Our study on alternative routes to excellence lends support to an educational philosophy of transcendence and inclusiveness. And so we say, let a
hundred flowers bloom; let a thousand flowers bloom; let a million flowers

bloom; for their petals shall mark the many and different routes that lead to excellence and high achievement.

Knowledge both reveals and conceals. All knowledge is partial; none has perfect knowledge. Therefore, we must be slow to limit access to knowledge because of the past experiences of individuals. We should never eliminate a path to excellence because it differs from the path most people travel.

III

FAMILY POWER AND DOMINANCE

7

Maternal Mentoring Models

Findings in the literature about parental identification suggest that "stronger father identification [is] associated with better adjustment and more masculine sex-role behavior of the son," according to Alfred Heilbrun Jr. (Heilbrun 1972: 59). Of women who have achieved in science and mathematics and in other areas, including professional athletics and the arts, Henry Biller's review of the literature informs us that "they are likely to have had fathers who did [not] stereotype them and gave them the strength to be able to deal with authority figures. . . . [Fathers] . . . helped them constructively deal with some of the barriers . . . in our society against women achieving" (Biller 1976: 76).

Not much has been written about mothers and their contribution to the career success of their children. It is fair to say that mothers have been ignored or denied. In the award-winning book *The American Occupational Structure*, authored by Peter Blau and Otis Duncan (1967), mothers largely were ignored. Beverly Duncan and Otis Dudley Duncan, analyzing data also collected in the study, reported that a factor favorable to occupational success among white men in two-parent families is a father who himself has been successful in the occupational sphere; "[but] among intact black families . . . the father's occupational achievement has only a slight influence on the occupational success of his male offspring" (Duncan and Duncan 1970: 168). These social scientists were silent about the effect, if any, of the activities of the mother in two-parent families on the occupational outcomes of offspring.

Much data have been accumulated on maternal deprivation. But such studies are concerned less with achievement outcomes of offspring than with the presence or absence of developmental deficiencies. Even some attempts at positive statements about mothers turn out to be negative: "There is evidence that indicates that father-absent children with competent mothers," according to Henry Biller, "are less likely to have certain types of developmental deficits than are children who have a dominating mother and a passive-ineffectual father" (Biller 1976: 70–71). Note that the earlier statements by Duncan and Duncan about the relationship of achievement of children and that of fathers did not mention mothers at all. But the Biller statement characterized dominant mothers as a socialization liability for children when these kinds of mothers are present in families with subdominant fathers. Nothing is said about the socialization effect on children of domineering fathers.

Blau and Duncan arranged for the collection of statistics on social mobility in a "Current Population Survey" of the U.S. Bureau of the Census. They developed a questionnaire that obtained information on male respondents and their parents, including the marital status of the respondent, items on the birthplace of the respondent, his father and mother, the educational attainment of the respondent's oldest brother (if any), the respondent's several occupations, the occupation of the respondent's father (or mother, if she headed a single-parent family), and, for a married respondent, the occupation of his father-in-law. To summarize, this study was concerned with the male respondent and then with a context variable—the education of the respondent's oldest brother but not that of the oldest sister, and the occupation of the respondent's father-in-law but not that of his mother-in-law. In two-parent families, the study ignored the occupational and educational attainments of the respondent's mother (Blau and Duncan 1967: 10–11).

With these data and their omissions, it is impossible to make any determination about characteristics of mothers and their association, if any, with the social mobility of offspring. Thus Blau and Duncan could state only that "father's occupational status . . . influences son's career achievement by affecting his education and first job [and] it also has a delayed effect on achievement that persists" (Blau and Duncan 1967: 40). They could say nothing about the mother's contribution to the offspring's career in two-parent families, the prevailing type.

If Blau and Duncan ignored mothers, Daniel Patrick Moynihan denied them. In his 1965 report to the nation on *The Negro Family*, Moynihan said, "White children without fathers at least perceive all about them the pattern of men working," but "Negro children without fathers flounder—and fail" (U.S. Labor Department 1965: 35). Young people, black as well as white, must have had mothers, but their existence and contribution to the educational and occupational success of their offspring is not mentioned by Moynihan. Only fathers or other men count in the career advancement or failure of young people, according to his assessment.

He concludes, "ours is a society which presumes male leadership in private and public affairs" (U.S. Labor Department 1965: 29). He also said, "a subculture, such as that of the Negro American, that does presume male leadership, is placed at a distinct disadvantage" (U.S. Labor Department 1965: 29). Indeed, Moynihan suggested that a family structure other than the one that presumes male leadership retards a population "because it is so out of line with the rest of the American society" (U.S. Labor Department 1965: 29). He was particularly negative about a matriarchal structure in which there is female leadership or domination. Moynihan's assertion seems to be a general denial of any significance of the contribution of mothers to the career development of their children and to the progress of a racial population.

Herbert Wasserman's study of poor black boys in Boston revealed no statistically significant differences in school performance of the sons in two-parent and in single-parent families. His study consisted of a sample of families in the same low-rent housing project that were similar in a number of background characteristics, including the ages of their male offspring (Wasserman 1970: 294–298). Although the Wasserman study did not identify a positive effect of mothers on the educational attainment of their children, it suggests the absence of a negative effect. Moynihan gave no evidence to support his contention that black children in single-parent households "fail and flounder." He was convinced, however, that there was "an unmistakable influence" (U.S. Labor Department 1965: 82).

In social science, there are agreed-upon canons that prescribe how data should be collected and analyzed. But what is studied often has autobiographical origins. For example, Blau and Duncan dedicated their book to their fathers "whose occupational achievements," they said, "greatly facilitated those of their [own]" (Blau and Duncan 1967: v). Believing that their fathers were essential to their success, Blau and Duncan designed a study that had, as a primary goal determining the association, if any, of fathers' achievements to those of their sons.

DEFINITION OF THE PROBLEM

The senior author, Charles Willie, is not immune from insinuating personal history into social science research. Growing up in a sexist society that, according to Moynihan, rewards males for being "dominant in family relationships" (U.S. Labor Department 1965: 29), Willie, too, thought that fathers were the more significant figures that facilitated the fashioning of a child's adult career, until he interviewed his mother and father in-depth after he became a professional sociologist.

In Charles Willie's family of orientation, the community-at-large heaped accolades upon his father—Louis James Willie Sr.—for the good job he did in providing for his family and in promoting the education of his children. With only an eighth-grade education, Willie's father left his homesite down on the farm in Panola County, Texas, and migrated to the city where he obtained a job with the Pullman Company—first in the Fort Worth district. He later transferred to the Dallas district of the company as a sleeping car porter. He was a steady worker and remained in the service of the Pullman Company for forty-two years, until his retirement. He was a thrifty person who did not squander his earnings. He was respected in the community and was goal-directed. He was an officer of the church and, for many years, its treasurer.

Willie's paternal grandparents were farmers. Before his paternal grandmother died, she asked Willie's father and his brothers to support the education of their only sister, the youngest child. In part to fulfill the request of his deceased mother, Willie's father left the farm and migrated to the city where he believed he could earn enough money to help send his sister to college. Willie's father left the farm and married Carrie Sykes. Louis James Willie Sr. and Carrie Sykes Willie met as youth delegates to a Sunday school convention in Marshall, Texas, her hometown. They lived together as husband and wife for more than fifty years, until Louis James Willie died in the late 1970s.

Marshall, Texas, where Carrie Sykes and her family lived, was a small town in East Texas near Panola County where Louise James Willie Sr. and his parents lived. She was the youngest member of her family and was the only one of several siblings to receive a college education. Willie's maternal grandfather was a blacksmith and his maternal grandmother was a cook in a private household. Willie's grandfather contracted for work at Wiley, a local college in Marshall, Texas, that needed a skilled blacksmith to help construct a men's dormitory. He requested that part of the funds owed him should be credited to a tuition account for Carrie, his youngest child.

Willie's mother was eager to go to school. She and her mother helped to raise tuition by taking in laundry for subsequent years after she was admitted to Wiley. His mother attended college for one semester a year for several years and did not graduate until she was thirty years old.

It was difficult for a married and educated woman to get work in a city school system during the Depression if her husband also had a job. Willie's father, of course, was employed as a Pullman porter. His mother wanted to work as a public schoolteacher, but the only jobs open to her were in rural counties far from her Dallas home. If Willie's mother had taken one of those jobs, she would have commuted home on weekends only. This arrangement would have increased family finances but weakened family bonds, owing to decreasing interaction between husband and wife and limited surveillance of four boys and a girl coming of age in a big-city ghetto.

Willie's mother and father decided that she would not work outside the home since she could not get a job in the local city school system. Explaining her decision to remain in continuous residence with her family, Carrie

Willie said that she was busy with the development of her "school at home," operated for the benefit of her husband and her five children. Willie's mother believed that if she could raise five good citizens of her community, of her state, and of her country, she would be doing more than if she left them to fend for themselves while she tried to teach the children of others in a distant community. This belief showed both her pragmatism and optimism. Willie said that his mother invented a Head Start program long before the 1960s when such a program was developed by the federal government.

Willie's mother and father made a joint decision that he would work for pay to provide the financial resources for the family and that she would work without pay as a homemaker, providing a supportive, learning environment for the family in her "school at home." The school-at-home theme was a manifestation of Willie's parents' belief in education, their orientation to the future, and their ability to transform liabilities into assets.

It is not uncommon for a working-class family to rally around one or two of the smarter youngsters in the household and send them to college. But, when all offspring in a relatively large working-class family with a modest income complete college and four of the five children obtain graduate degrees, something unusual must be happening. Such was the experience of Willie and his siblings.

What Willie recognized as a significant contribution to the family's achievement during the interviews with his parents was the extraordinary capacities of his mother. Her educational attainment was unusual for a black woman of her background who was born before the twentieth century. Her training was higher than that of her husband. Moreover, her occupational status, if the local school system had hired her, would have been as a professional teacher, an occupation also outranking that of Willie's father as a service worker. Apparently, the educational and occupational capacities of Carrie Willie enhanced and did not undercut the role of her husband in the family. This finding is contrary to assertions by some social scientists about the negative effects of a female spouse of achievement who is task-oriented (U.S. Department of Labor 1965: 34). In addition, there appeared to be an association between the educational attainment of mother Willie, a college graduate, and that of her offspring, all of whom are college graduates.

In 1973, three years before *Roots* was published (Haley 1976), Willie took his tape recorder in hand and flew from his residence in Syracuse, New York, where he was a university teacher and administrator to Dallas, Texas, to visit with his parents. They were in their early eighties. Willie wanted to hear from them the specifics of their story—how they managed to do so much for their offspring with so little.

In these conversations, he discovered that his father and mother were a team but that she really was the foundation of the family and contributed enormously to the achievement of its members. In unobtrusive ways, she supported and sustained the efforts of her husband and her children. She was the auditor and accountant of family finances, speechwriter for her husband, tutor and storyreader for her children, nursemaid for the sick, purchasing agent and consumer advocate for the best bargains in the marketplace, director of recreation and celebrant for holidays, cook, laundry person, disciplinarian, cleaning lady, and a quiet cheerleader for all; she and Willie's father were a team. And without her, what happened would not have happened the way that it did.

Recognizing his mother as a significant contributor to her children's and husband's achievement, Willie questioned whether or not other mothers have played this fundamental role but have been ignored or denied. In addition to recognizing in adulthood what his mother did for him and his brothers and sister as children, which he did not understand as a child, he also was persuaded to believe that part of his father's indomitable drive to educate all of his children was, in part, a spillover from the promise he made to his mother on her deathbed that he would find a way to help send his young sister to college.

Willie's experience has been that mothers, whether in life or in death, are formidable influences. The thought occurred to him that in his interviews he had done more than capture the history of his own family. He had, in the words of the book jacket writer for *Roots*, "rediscovered for an entire people a rich cultural heritage." Indeed, his search for the full role of mothers in the achievement of their offspring may speak "not just to blacks, or to whites, but to all people" (Haley 1976, book jacket). We can verify these assertions about the contributions of mothers only if we stop ignoring or denying them in our research designs and analyses. Reflecting upon his personal experiences caused him to hypothesize that mothers play a significant role in the achievement of many offspring. Willie was particularly interested in the role of mothers in households in which the mother has as much or more education than her husband and works outside the home or is inclined to do so. Some mothers differed from the stereotype of the passive female who needs a dominating male to watch over her. Indeed, Robert Leik's finding regarding interaction within families (that mothers are more task-oriented in the family [Leik 1972: 265]), caused Willie to wonder whether his mother's contribution to the achievement of her household was normative and not unique.

REVIEW OF THE LITERATURE

A review of the literature revealed an interesting finding about mothers that was similar to Willie's personal experience. James Morgan and associates at the University of Michigan discovered that "[educational] attainment of both parents appear to stimulate education of children," and that "where the wife has less education than [her husband], achievements of the children are impeded but not so much as [achievements of the children] are advanced when the wife has more education than [her husband]." (Morgan 1962: 374–75). In the light of this finding, we have been careful to design our social science investigations about career development and social mobility so that they obtain information on mothers as well as fathers.

The study about which we wish to give a partial report is a case analysis of the interrelationship of career advancement, educational attainment, and the family life of five outstanding black scholars in history, psychology, political science, economics, and literature (Willie 1986). All of the scholars are male because the study was of the most outstanding black scholar in each field as determined by vote of their peers. In a sexist society, the most outstanding scholar has a greater probability of being male, owing to the extraordinary opportunities that have been accorded to men compared to those accorded women.

CASE STUDIES

John Hope Franklin, Harvard Ph.D., historian, professor emeritus of the University of Chicago, former president of the Southern Historical Association, the American Historical Association, and the United Chapters of Phi Beta Kappa, came from a professional family; his parents were college graduates. His father studied and practiced law. However, his practice experienced several reversals owing to racial discrimination, a race riot, and the Depression. When their father was away attempting to establish his law practice in Tulsa, Oklahoma, John Hope Franklin and his siblings remained at home with his mother, who was a schoolteacher in Rentiesville, Oklahoma—an all-black town of about two thousand people. His father eventually relocated the family in Tulsa. Before that happened, young Franklin was in the full care and company of his mother most of the time. Young Franklin accompanied his schoolteacher mother to school, sat on the back bench in her classes, and was told to be quiet. As he quietly played on the back bench, he also heard her instructions to others and learned to read at an early age. Such early learning gave Franklin a head start.

W. Arthur Lewis, a knight of the United Kingdom with a Ph.D. in economics from the London School of Economics, had been a faculty member in British and American universities. Now deceased, he was professor emeritus at the Woodrow Wilson School, Princeton University. Lewis was a former president of a university and a bank, and he was elevated by his peers to the offices of vice president and president of the American Economics Association.

Born in the British West Indies to parents who were educated in a two-year normal school for the preparation of teachers in Antigua, Lewis experienced the death of his father, a teacher, when he was only seven years old. His mother gave up teaching after marriage but returned to the labor force as a businesswoman after the death of her husband. She operated a dry goods enterprise. She supported and sustained five children on the income from the business. All offspring, five sons, received higher education. Some were sent to England to study law, medicine, and economics. Of his widowed mother, Sir Arthur Lewis said, "I never found out how she managed to establish and support us; but she did, on the income from the business" (Willie 1986: 31). In effect, she provided an umbrella of safety and security for the members of her family until they departed from the household to go to college.

Psychologist Kenneth B. Clark received his Ph.D. from Columbia University. Former president of the American Psychological Association, Clark has been an activist scholar, searching for justice and equality. For nearly two decades he served as a member of the powerful Board of Regents that established educational policy for the State of New York. The significant Supreme Court decision of *Brown v. Board of Education* that outlawed segregated education in the United States referred to the psychological research findings of Clark.

A loyal member of the faculty of the City University of New York for a third of a century, Clark retired as distinguished university professor emeritus. A member of Phi Beta Kappa, Clark was the first recipient of the Award for Distinguished Contribution to Psychology in the Public Interest.

Clark attributes his success to two women in his life—his mother and his wife. When the marriage between his mother and father broke up, his mother moved with her infant daughter and four-year-old son from the Panama Canal Zone, where the children were born, to New York City to be near a sister who already lived there and also to find better educational opportunities for her children. Clark's mother obtained work in the garment district as a dressmaker. She worked and took care of her family during the day, went to school at night, and eventually received a high school diploma. She insisted that her son be accepted in an academic program rather than being steered to a vocational high school as was customary for blacks in the days of Clark's youth. Clark said that his mother insisted on these arrangements because she was not afraid of authority; her daring ways, he said, saved him and his sisters. She also demanded good grades from her son and told him that he had to go to college but left the choice of college up to him. She told him that he would get good grades or that he would end up in jail. Amused as he reflected upon this, Clark said, "She didn't give me any middle ground." He had some scholarship money and did not have to work his way through college. His mother gave full support. She worked to put him and his sister through college, and she also provided some support for graduate school.

Clark characterized both his mother and his wife as strong women who demanded from him the maximum. Clark and his family of orientation persevered under adverse circumstances and eventually overcame.

Matthew Holden Jr., a political scientist with a Ph.D. degree from Northwestern University, was born in Mound Bayou, Mississippi, an all-black town. In the Carter administration, he was commissioner of the Federal Energy Regulatory Commission. He has been a professor at the University of Wisconsin and now occupies an endowed chair in political science at the University of Virginia. He is past vice president of the American Political Science Association and has served as an elected member of its Council. In Wisconsin, he was a high-level public administrator in state government.

Holden remained in Mississippi until the age of thirteen; then his family migrated to Chicago in search of work, because of crop failures on the farm. On the farm, Holden took his turn in the field chopping and picking cotton. He was surrounded by an extended family, including his grandparents and several aunts, uncles, and cousins.

Holden's father completed the fifth grade and his mother the eleventh grade. Both worked outside the home. They held semiskilled and laboring jobs in Chicago but wanted their offspring to achieve more. Going to college, said Holden, was as preordained as anything could be. Although Holden worked the fields with his family, they never permitted him to miss school for any reason except illness. Holden believed that his parents' interest in his attending college fulfilled wishes of his paternal family for his uncle who attended college but died before finishing and those of his mother who wanted to go to college but was denied that opportunity. Holden's extended family said that he was smart like his uncle who died. Family members, therefore, transferred the hopes and ambitions they had for his uncle to him. Holden described his mother as an extremely intelligent woman who always read the newspaper and the Bible. She wanted to go to Rust College in Mississippi and had a patron who offered to send her, but her father would not accept what he called charity. Later, however, he apologized to his daughter, Holden's mother, for not letting her go to college under the available arrangement.

Holden's parents eventually separated after moving to Chicago. He remained a member of his mother's household until he received a master's degree. Of his mother, he said, "I could always count on her." She nurtured him through the doubting years of adolescence and provided a safe and secure shelter to which he could return after his probes into the outside world. There was bread enough in his mother's household but not much of anything else to share. Holden's parents, who were blue-collar workers, supported him through six years of stop-and-go studies at two colleges for a college education. His mother, in particular, stood by him despite his undistinguished undergraduate career.

Darwin Turner, now deceased, a specialist in literary criticism, received his doctorate degree from the University of Chicago. A member of Phi Beta Kappa, Turner held a tenured distinguished professorship of English and was director of the Afro-American Studies program at the University of Iowa. He shuttled back and forth between administration and scholarship in his career. In recognition of his scholarly attainment, Turner was given the Creative Scholarship Award by the College Language Association and was presented the University of Chicago Alumni Association's Professional Achievement Award. A former member of the Board of Directors of the Modern Language Association, Turner also served as a trustee of the National Humanities Center.

Turner grew up in an extended family of highly educated individuals. His grandfather and grandmother earned degrees for graduate study. In fact, his grandmother, a public school principal, received her graduate degree the same year that her daughter (Turner's mother and also a public school educator) received her graduate degree. Turner's father, a college graduate, pursued graduate studies, but he did not receive a doctoral degree. He shifted to formal training in pharmacy and became a pharmacist and business manager.

Turner said that his mother and grandmother encouraged him in school. One could say they doted on him. His grandmother offered him a dollar for every A that he received. His mother promised him a car if he was elected to Phi Beta Kappa. Turner does not recall that these promises were kept. But he remembers them as incentives and as statements of expectations.

His family was solid middle class and was able to pay for his education. Turner remembers that his grandmother especially wanted him to go on immediately for the Ph.D. degree after he received his M.A. degree, but he said that he had other things on his mind—getting married and going to work.

Turner grew up in a two-parent household in Cincinnati. However, his father found business opportunities better in Chicago and moved there to establish three pharmacies. His father and mother visited each other often. But Turner remained with his mother and his extended family in Cincinnati. Later, while studying for the doctorate degree at the University of Chicago, Turner and his new family had closer contact with his father.

ANALYSIS OF THE CASES

These case studies, reported in part, do not deny the role of fathers, but they certainly emphasize the contributions of mothers as significantly related to the success of their offspring. After analyzing the lives of these outstanding scholars, one is tempted to hypothesize that the educational and occupational careers of mothers greatly facilitate those of their children. We know this because, unlike other investigations, we studied the contributions of both mothers and fathers. The mothers in this study gave constant company, care, head-start learning opportunities, and partial or full economic support for offspring, including funds for education. They expected good academic performance, had ambitions for the high achievement of their offspring, were patient when the young faltered, provided incentives for good academic work, and expressed hope for success in the future.

The outstanding scholars in this study grew up in different kinds of households. All five experienced two-parent families initially. But three of the scholars saw their families disintegrate before they came of age—one because of death and two because of divorce or desertion. Two of the scholars had intensive interaction in extended kinship units. Even in the two-parent families that remained so, during childhood two of the scholars experienced temporary separations between the parents because of the father's work in distant communities. These scholars, therefore, came of age in a variety of kinship structures, including nuclear families, extended families, and single-parent families. No ideal type of common family form was revealed.

Despite a variety of family structures, the presence and encouragement of mothers were common experiences for all scholars. A similar characteristic of these mothers was their labor force participation. All worked for some period after the birth of children in jobs ranging from unskilled work to business administration and professional activity. The kind of work the mothers performed is less important than the fact that they were available to work, if needed. In four of the households studied, the income of the mothers was essential in providing safe and secure environments for offspring and educational opportunities for children. Thus, it would appear that parental expectations and support for young people in the family as well as mentoring and role modeling were significant factors that contributed to the children's success.

Finally, this study of five outstanding scholars confirms the hypothesis set forth by James Morgan and his associates at the University of Michigan (Morgan 1962). Although the mothers attained varying levels of education ranging from the eleventh grade of high school to certification from a teacher-training school to baccalaureate and master's degrees, in four of the families the mothers received as much (or more) education as their husbands. And, of course, the offspring in all five families received doctoral degrees.

CONFIRMATION OF OTHER STUDIES

Some years ago, Willie conducted a study of a sample of low-income black families and families slightly above the poverty line to determine how the latter families pulled themselves out of poverty, since husbands in all families were unskilled workers who received low wages. About one-third of all families in the sample had climbed out of poverty largely because of the work of the fe-male spouse. Three out of every four wives in the households slightly above the poverty line were employed, compared with the poor households in which three out of every four wives were not employed. The working wives in the households above the poverty line tended to earn as much as their husbands or more. But the few employed women in the poor household earned signifi-cantly less than their male spouses.

A fact possibly related to the earning power of the wives in families above the poverty line was their education. Nearly half of these wives were high school graduates, compared with only one-fourth of the wives in poor households. Moreover, a greater proportion of wives than husbands in households above the poverty line were high school graduates compared with those in the poor households. Thus, in this study, households that had risen out of poverty by their own "bootstraps" did so because of the educa-tional and occupational attainments of the wife (Willie 1981).

The findings of this study of poor families and those slightly above the poverty line, and the case studies of five outstanding scholars, suggest that Moynihan's assertion that "dependence on the mother's income undermines the position of the father and deprives the children" is in error (U.S. Depart-ment of Labor 1965: 25).

Studies of black middle-class families reported in an earlier edition of this book revealed the economic foundation of most to be a product of the co-operative work of husband and wife, a genuine illustration of a team effort: Few, if any, family functions including cooking, cleaning, and shopping are considered to be the exclusive prerogative of the husband or wife. This in-formation leads us to the conclusion that probably the best example of the liberated wife in American society is found in the black middle-class family. This is so because she and her husband have acted as partners out of neces-sity and thus have carved out an equalitarian pattern of interaction in which neither husband nor wife has ultimate authority. This equalitarian existence that permits full participation of the wife and mother in the family and in other community institutions is beneficial for the personal growth and de-velopment of the male as well as the female spouse and presumably for their children, as the study of five outstanding scholars has revealed. It could be that neither a matriarchal nor a patriarchal family structure is appropriate for the mutual fulfillment of family members—that an equalitarian structure is better for all concerned.

NEED FOR FURTHER RESEARCH

We are mindful that most studies reported here are of blacks, including black scholars and their families. Their way of life also has been ignored or denied. When acknowledged, the adaptation patterns of blacks have been studied largely as a form of deviance from the mainstream of social organization. This discussion should help us to develop a different perspective on the value of differential adaptations of families in dominant and subdominant racial populations.

With a broader perspective than the one limited to social problems analysis, we are better able to conduct comparative studies of family life, which should be high on our research agenda. Willie's comparative study of black and white families in the United States has, as one of its goals, the determination of whether the adaptations discovered among blacks also apply to whites and whether equalitarian patterns of interaction found in the black middle class extends also to other social classes and to these classes in different racial populations (Willie 1985). Finally, the comparative analysis seeks to determine whether the contribution of mothers to the achievement of male offspring holds also for fathers with reference to the achievement of daughters (Appleton 1981: 71–103; Biller 1974; Hennig and Jardin 1976). The outcome of research on the role of fathers in the lives of women of achievement will be reported in the next chapter.

8

Paternal Mentoring Models

Coauthored by Jolene Lane

For several years, we have reviewed the literature and have attempted to understand the interaction dynamic within families. The literature review has revealed only partial information about family adaptations because sociologists, like journalists, are more inclined to document social problems rather than successes. Much has been written about the negative consequences for children when parents default on fulfilling their roles. We need to know, also, about the positive effects for sons and daughters when mothers and fathers function in appropriate and proper ways.

Many discussions about offspring and the contributions parents make to their lives have to do largely with fathers and their sons or mothers and their daughters (Foreman 1993: 1, 12; Friday 1977). Mothers are seldom discussed in studies of the success of sons. To correct this omission of information, chapter 7, "The Mother's Role in Male Achievement," was included in the book. Reported were findings of a small study in which mothers were significantly related to the success of their male offspring. Despite living in a variety of family structures, including single-parent, two-parent, and extended-family households, encouragement by mothers was a common experience for all of the black male scholars discussed in chapter 7.

Fathers, and particularly black fathers, are seldom mentioned in studies of the adaptation of women. Jill Ker Conway's book *Written by Herself* (1992) reports on the lives of women "which can't be crammed into conventional cultural categories" (Conway 1992: x). She "present[s] the most powerful female voices commenting on the American experience" (Conway 1992: xii). Her book begins with the story of four black women: Harriet Ann Jacobs, Zora Neal Hurston, Marian Anderson, and Maya Angelou.

In the introduction to these excerpts of autobiographical essays, Conway states that "the [black] men in these stories come and go" and that they are "uncertain quantities" (Conway 1992: 4). Conway arrives at this conclusion despite Harriet Ann Jacob's testimony that her early childhood years in slavery in the household of her mother and father were happy and that her father's "strongest wish was to purchase his children['s] freedom and on several occasions offered his hard earnings [from working as a carpenter] for that purpose [but] . . . never succeeded" (Conway 1992: 7). Conway's conclusion ignores Zora Neale Hurston's statement that it was her stepmother who "resented Papa's tender indulgence for his older daughter, [Sarah];" Conway's conclusion is contrary to Marian Anderson's memory that the whole family "looked forward to [her father's] homecoming every evening" from his job at the Reading Terminal Market and that he took her to church every Sunday "partly . . . to alleviate [her] mother's burden of taking care of three children" (Conway 1992: 55). Three out of four concerned fathers isn't bad and does not merit the generalization that black men are "uncertain quantities" in black families.

Margaret Hennig and Anne Jardin presented evidence that fathers as well as mothers play important roles in the successful careers of their daughters in the study, *The Managerial Woman* (1976). Twenty-five white women in this study reached top management positions in business. All said that they had "close relationships with their fathers" and that their fathers took them to visit various places, praised and encouraged them, and instructed them never to let others impose limits on their level of achievement (Hennig and Jardin 1976: 99–108).

Contrary to Conway's conclusion and based on a review of the experiences of Jacob, Hurston, and Anderson with their fathers and the Hennig and Jardin study, we assumed that some black fathers are helpful in the career development of their daughters as are some white fathers. Thus, we decided to study a small sample of outstanding black women to determine the effects, if any, of fathers on their achievement.

METHOD AND DATA

The life history case study method was chosen as most appropriate to examine this matter. This method, according to Robert Bogdan and Sari Biklen, "[uses] the person as a vehicle to understand basic aspects of human behavior" (Bogdon and Biklen 1982: 61). They further state that "sociological life histories often try to construct subjects' careers emphasizing the role of . . . crucial events and significant others in shaping [their] evolving definition of self and their perspectives on life" (Bogdan and Biklen 1982: 61). We were particularly interested in the life histories of successful black women who had vivid memories of how they interacted with their parents during childhood and adolescent years.

Rannveig Traustadottir has questioned the efficacy "of approaching family studies with a gender-blind approach that makes invisible the difference between mothers' and fathers' experiences within families" (Traustadottir 1991: 226). This study does not deny that the adaptation of daughters may be influenced by the actions of their mothers. However, it focuses on fathers and daughters, since their interaction has not been examined in depth in social science literature.

A provisional hypothesis for this study is that there is a cross-gender parental effect with respect to the achievement of offspring—that fathers have a major influence as mentors on successful daughters and that mothers have a major influence as mentors on successful sons. This study has to do with achievement levels that are classified as outstanding. The hypothesis is grounded in findings reported in *Five Black Scholars* (Willie 1986) and in *The Managerial Woman* (Hennig and Jardin 1976). As indicated by Anselm L. Strauss, "a case history can be very useful if brought into very close conjunction with a grounded theory" (Strauss 1987: 221).

Over a period of three years in the early 1980s, Emily Wilson, whom Maya Angelou calls "a good and recognized poet," and Susan Mullally, a photographer, traveled on highways and byways of North Carolina talking to older black women and listening to their stories. Part of their goal was to document the achievement of women, especially women previously unrecognized. Angelou states that the twenty-seven women presented in Wilson's and Mullally's book, *Hope and Dignity: Older Black Women of the South* (1983), are "authentic voices" (1983: book jacket and xii). Angelou's statement about the authenticity of the "voices" in a case study is similar to a statement made by Samuel Stouffer, a famous methodologist in sociology. He said that "the case history provides a sequence of events in their cultural setting" and that "a classification of these sequences into types, even if the research is based on a smaller number of cases[,] . . . should be a fruitful approach to . . . interpretation . . . [;] in particular, it should give clues to connection links" (Stouffer 1980: 52).

Although she is identified as a poet, Emily Wilson used data-gathering methods that are similar to those used in ethnographic research. This is her description: "Sometimes our visits lasted only several hours. On many occasions, we were able to come back for several days of talking. We have known a dozen of the women in frequent visits, telephone conversations, and letters. Each time we returned, we learned more, often changing first impressions; sometimes the women asked to go back to an earlier question in order to tell us more than they had been willing to tell during the first visit" (Wilson and Mullally 1983: xxi).

Wilson and her photographer are white. However, she states, they were "warmly welcomed in the homes" visit after visit. "If our visits started out with an awkward formality, they ended with laughter and good will." Wilson also tells of her failed attempts to obtain some interviews and of a few hostile reactions to her because of her race. In general, she reports that a friendly and cooperative relationship was achieved between the researcher and most of the black women interviewed. Wilson and her photographer believe that because of the relationship established with most of the women they met, they were told "the truth" (Wilson and Mullally 1983).

Women selected from the Wilson study for this secondary analysis are of high-level occupational achievement. Their biographies include material on their relationships with their mothers and fathers. These women had successful careers in business administration, education, publishing, and social service administration. By studying a small sample of black women of achievement, it is clear that their life histories are similar, in some ways, to those of the five outstanding black male scholars that were studied and reported in chapter 7.

These are the five black women selected for an analysis of their life histories: Beatrice Garrett Burnett of Tarboro, North Carolina, was a physical education teacher in the Tarboro Public School System, a political activist, and organized a local chapter of the National Association for the Advancement of Colored People (NAACP); Lyda Moore Merrick of Durham, North Carolina, founded and edited *The Merrick/Washington Magazine for the Blind*, a national publication directed toward the needs of black people with sight impairments; Ernestine Burghes Saunders of Raleigh, North Carolina, a college professor of French at St. Augustine College, studied at the Sorbonne in France; Viola Mitchell Turner of Durham, North Carolina, retired from North Carolina Mutual Life Insurance Company as financial vice president and was a member of the Board of Directors; and Madie Hall Xuma of Winston-Salem, North Carolina, an educator and social service administrator, worked as a Young Women's Christian Association (YWCA) executive and organizer among blacks in Lynchburg, Virginia, Winston-Salem, North Carolina, and Johannesburg, South Africa. She also served eight years on the Executive Board of the world organization of the YWCA. Of Wilson's twenty-seven case studies, three other women were eligible for our study because of their high achievement, but they were excluded. In one case, exclusion was invoked because it was a study of three sisters rather than the study of a single individual. Another case was excluded because insufficient information was given about the person's work life, and a third case was excluded because insufficient information was available about the father in the family.

While the women studied were not randomly selected, no criteria were used to exclude participants in this study other than an incomplete biography and nonprofessional or nonmanagerial employment. The criteria for inclusion and exclusion would appear to be legitimate for a study of women of achievement and their families of orientation. All of the interviewees had retired when the study was conducted and were able to reflect on a full and successful life. Thus, they were able to talk about significant individuals, important events, and the connections between these events and individuals that contributed to their success.

In social science, there is a tendency to use the terms mentor and role model interchangeably. Conceptually, we make a distinction in this study. Role models are people whose behavior we imitate, while mentors are people who serve as our advocates. While one individual may be both role model and mentor, often these functions are performed by different people. In the context of the provisional hypothesis stated earlier, this analysis will confirm or cast doubt on the contention that black women of achievement tend to turn to their fathers as mentors. An additional hypothesis worthy of future study is that black women of achievement also tend to turn toward their mothers as role models.

FINDINGS

Beatrice Garrett Burnett

Beatrice Burnett graduated from Elizabeth City State Normal School and began teaching in the public schools of Tarboro in 1912 at the age of nineteen. For more than fifty years, she introduced children to games and sports. She organized extracurricular recreation and team sports in her school and community. She took advanced courses at Hampton Institute and other colleges and universities almost every summer. "I hadn't had any particular training for physical education. I was interested in all kinds of sports, but mostly basketball, and when I began working, I taught basketball."

Because no man had been hired to teach basketball to the seventh-grade boys, the only way they could play basketball was the way Burnett taught them. Later, they would tell her "if it hadn't been for you we couldn't have made the high school team!" Mrs. Burnett proudly stated, "I had some girls [who] could do anything the boys could do." Beatrice Burnett had tremendous support from her school principal to initiate new things. She once bought a soccer ball with her own money. "But the ball didn't cost that much. I went to Hampton, learned soccer, came back and introduced this game to my seventh grade class in 1929. I'd just go on out and go to summer school so I could learn something new to pass on to my children."

Mrs. Burnett was not only a teacher of physical education; she used physical education and fitness as tools for teaching. "When I first began following the Olympics, Jesse Owens won the decathlon. So I told my children, 'you don't know any more about the Olympics than I do, so you go look it up. Let's go back to the beginning and see how it started and where it started and all of that. Then hereafter, when you see the games and when we hear this expression or that expression, we'll know just what's happening.'" When Burnett was teaching eighth grade, Wilma Rudolph won three gold medals. That was interesting because at one time she couldn't walk. "I said, 'So, see, children, there's no point in giving up. Don't ever give up. If Wilma could overcome that handicap, you can do anything. You can overcome anything.'"

The community paid great tribute to Beatrice Burnett for her lifetime of leadership and service in physical fitness, education, and recreation by naming the gymnasium of the Tarboro City recreation center in her honor. All the while she was teaching and coaching, Mrs. Burnett was active in the NAACP, serving as president of the Tarboro chapter for seventeen years and holding state and national positions. More than any other person, she is responsible for the establishment and growth of the NAACP in eastern North Carolina. She organized the first Youth Council in 1948. This is one of her greatest sources of pride because the young people raised their own money and initiated a voter registration campaign in 1958. They increased substantially the number of registered black voters.

As Beatrice Burnett reflected on the influence of her father in her life, she said that she stood firmly in her father's footsteps, he was "a politician from the sole of his feet to the top of his head." Recalling her father's words, she remembered that he often said, "You're as good as anybody else. I'm as good as the President. The President has one vote, and I have one vote." That was a remarkable philosophy of life by which she was raised.

After the passage of the Nineteenth Amendment in 1920, Beatrice Burnett, her sister, and a physician's wife were the first women—"I don't mean just black women"—to register to vote in the town of Tarboro. "And the man who was the registrar said, 'I knew you were coming because I know your father wouldn't let you live in that house [without registering] after this law went through.'" Mrs. Burnett's father taught her strength of will and character. Reflecting on her lifetime in politics and physical education, she emphasized that "What I have done, I have done because of the inspiration my father gave me. He was born in slavery time, but he was not quite six when the Civil War ended." Beatrice Burnett's paternal grandfather was the shoemaker on the plantation. After he had produced the shoes for that plantation, the master would hire him out to other plantations as well. He was sent away when Burnett's father was an infant barely crawling, and they never saw him again. His mother reared her children on her own, and "she was one of those like my father that didn't take anything from anybody."

Beatrice Burnett's father was born in Princeville, "[one of] the oldest incorporated colored towns in the United States (February 12, 1885). It was called Freedom Hill because most of the people who lived in Princeville then were born in slavery time." Her father was reared on a farm, and when he and the family moved to town, "he went directly into politics. He was also a businessman and he was in business on Main Street from 1895 until he died in 1928. His leadership encouraged at least ten other blacks to go into business on Main Street. He reared seven children. Everything that we have, all the education that we have, came through that business."

> My father was elected to the General Assembly, but he wasn't seated. When the votes were counted for him, they wouldn't count any of the votes of blacks. But I tell you what, he was the [elected] magistrate in our county and served as magistrate two terms. He was in everything, and he voted. My mother said she'd let my father do the politicking. But she'd stick right behind him in anything he wanted to do.

Beatrice Garrett Burnett's narrative expressed stories that made clear her commitment to family and community that actualized her quest to work to elect leaders "who will do the most for my people."

Lyda Moore Merrick

By birth, Lyda Merrick is a member of one of North Carolina's most prominent black families. Her marriage in 1916 to Ed Merrick remarkably created an alliance between two of the most powerful black families in the state. Her father, Dr. A. M. Moore, and her father-in-law, John Merrick, were among the founders of the North Carolina Mutual and Provident Association in 1898, one of the oldest black-owned businesses in the nation. This business later became the North Carolina Mutual Life Insurance Company, one of the largest black-owned companies in the United States.

The distinguished legacy of Dr. Aaron McDuffie Moore, who became the first black physician in Durham, North Carolina, in 1888, reveals how the enterprises of the father imbued his daughter with a family mission of public service. Lyda Merrick carried the torch for public service her father gave to her. Dr. Moore founded Lincoln Hospital in 1901 and the Colored Library in 1913, and he led the movement for the improvement of rural schools for black children in North Carolina. Lyda Merrick came from a family tradition of enterprise, political activism, community service, and commitment to education.

Her narrative shows how she was influenced by her father. She said, "My father passed a torch to me which I have never let go out. We are blessed to serve." Her family customs are anchored in southern black history, yet they are permeated with purposeful change. Her father's goal was to further his education, and "he was a student all his life." His education began "down in the country where he was born, but he realized its inadequacy and kept trying to further his education. His intention was to be a teacher when he matriculated at Shaw University, which had a medical program, too. The program had just opened the year before he came to Shaw. He entered the medical class because "[it] seemed very important to him that blacks should have access to physicians."

Lyda Merrick described her mother as "very smart, artistic. . . . She was a great church worker, and she was a club woman, federated clubs." She also had a good understanding about business.

Mrs. Merrick's father was a physician, dentist, entrepreneur, Sunday school superintendent, foster parent, and innkeeper. "My mother was behind my father in everything he did." Merrick's parents had a very egalitarian relationship and they worked together on many projects. Merrick described their house as an underground railroad. "They all came up here from the country to stay in our house. We had a spare room. Papa was always bringing somebody to our house. He'd brought them from the country and fix them up city-like, and we had a very happy home. They were so grateful for what he was doing for them, and Papa saw that they got their schooling."

When Lyda Merrick and her sister finished school, their father took them on a cross-country journey without their mother to the World's Fair in San Francisco in 1915. It was a profound experience that stirred his daughters' intellects as well as their souls. This father-daughter journey laid the foundation for adventure that Lyda Merrick maintained throughout her life. Dr. Moore turned their trip into a month-long lesson in geography, history, and life, despite the indignity of discrimination they experienced in a few places on their journey. Lyda Moore Merrick cherished that excursion with her father and the new things that she learned. She likened the world of the blind to the world of southern blacks that was closed to these new experiences. "With some of our people, suffering has made finer souls, coming out pure gold. They have created for themselves a beautiful world." Lyda Merrick thought that those people deserved more; she discovered a way to enhance their knowledge.

Lyda Merrick's offering took the form of the *Merrick/Washington Magazine for the Blind*, founded in 1952 as *The Negro Braille Magazine*. She was editor of the magazine for eighteen years; throughout her career, she dedicated her service to finding endowment funds for the magazine to guarantee that it would survive and thrive. Based on her father's simple wish ("If only my people had something to read!"), Lyda Merrick believed that she was destined to create the Braille magazine "to give the Negro blind a bridge between themselves and the sighted world." From her father's entrepreneurial spirit, she obtained the inspiration to start her own projects and invested in their continued success. Because of her lifelong relationship with a friend who was born blind, she first created Lincoln Library's Corner for the blind, and later began the Braille magazine.

Ernestine Burghes Saunders

Ernestine Saunders was an only child and she admits, "I was my father's heart." Her father was the Reverend John R. Burghes, a Methodist minister, who was born in Mississippi but whose parents moved to Selma, Alabama. Her father lived in a German settlement and spoke German as a boy. "He was a product of what we call the tragic situation of the South at that time." Frequently, the children born in the first generation after slavery were illegitimate. Though he never told her, his daughter guessed that her paternal grandfather was German.

"My mother went to the first black school that was established in Selma, Burrell Normal School. That would have been in the late 1890s." The principal of the school was later transferred to Talladage College, "and because my mother was a good student, the principal asked my grandfather to let her go with him." Ernestine Burghes Saunders' mother attended Talladega College for one year, and, after passing an examination in Selma, she was certified to teach. She taught English for three years until she married the Reverend John Burghes. Ernestine Saunders remembered that during her school days, her mother would help with literature assignments, while her father would help with foreign language and math assignments. She said, "Before I began my study of languages, I had my first lessons with my father."

She attended Miles College in Birmingham, Alabama, and finished what was the equivalent of junior college. While at Miles, one of the teachers made the remark that women could not learn Greek. The next day Ernestine Saunders enrolled in a Greek class. There were four young men in that class. After completing Miles, she attended Fisk University. In 1928, she joined the faculty at Talladega College where she taught French, German, and Spanish for seventeen years. During the final twenty-three years of her career, Ernestine Saunders was an associate professor at St. Augustine's College in Raleigh, North Carolina.

Ernestine Burghes Saunders had many magnificent accomplishments. She continually pursued further education and knowledge, which she shared with her many students. This lifelong commitment to continuing education resulted in a master's degree from Middlebury College in Vermont and graduate studies at Northwestern University, the Sorbonne in France, Columbia University, and the University of North Carolina at Chapel Hill.

Mrs. Saunders' recollection of her father was that of a very loving and devoted man. Their relationship was extremely close and he always supported and encouraged his daughter. "I graduated from Fisk in 1926, and I was one of the senior orators based on my grades. . . . My father was at my graduation. My mother didn't come. She loved me just as much, but he had a particular sort of closeness to me. When I went to Fisk, he took me there. When

I went to Miles, he took me there. I was the only child, so everything I did was alright with them."

Viola Mitchell Turner

Viola Mitchell Turner reminisced about her childhood: "I had a lovely childhood, poor—I didn't know it, however—but very lovely." She was an only child growing up in Macon, Georgia. Her parents married at the age of fifteen, and she was born when they were sixteen years old. Her father was a cotton sampler from the early fall to the late spring, and a hotel man from the spring through the summer. She described her mother as "a very smart, little lady. She was aggressive, ambitious, and determined. That's all I heard all of my life, 'You've got to go to school. Stay in school.' My father was a sweet, loving man. Nobody had a dearer father than I had. He gave me lots of attention. . . . But my father, I'm quite sure, didn't see the point in all the education my mother was talking about. It was okay. If she wanted me to go to school, it was okay [with him]."

Viola Turner attended the American Missionary Association School because there was not a public school for blacks in Macon. After graduating, she enrolled in the business department of Morris Brown College in Atlanta, Georgia. After completing Morris Brown, she was employed for a year as a secretary at Tuskegee Institute. She worked for a short time for the State Office of Negro Education, and she was ultimately hired by the North Carolina Mutual Life Insurance Company. Viola Turner's knowledge of investments made her one of the best-known women on Wall Street. When she retired in 1865, she held the position of financial vice president and she was a member of the board of directors in the insurance company, the first woman elected to such a high post in the company.

Mrs. Turner was essentially self-taught in the financial field because she was willing to take risks and she was not shy about asking difficult questions. She timed her entry into the investment field perfectly because no one in the company knew anything about investments. Mrs. Turner began to ask relevant questions, to educate herself, and to create a library of information in the company. Because she was extremely impressive in this largely male field, she made many connections and became well-respected and well-known. The brokers discovered a black woman who knew the terminology of the financial world and could maneuver comfortably and effortlessly within it.

"I could be wrong, but I didn't think too many men would call in and ask for something and say, 'Look, I'm stumped. I don't know what the heck to do with this. What do you think?' Even if they want the information, they're not going to ask for it. They're going to talk all around and sound intelligent, and think that maybe in the course of the conversation they'll get the answer." Mrs. Turner was always willing to ask for information, and she received prompt and thorough answers. Viola Turner believed that she understood the dynamic of being a woman in a male-dominated field. "This may be an unkind observation, but it's one I had then, and I don't think I've changed it at all. Our men are not too happy about [women] being too intelligent. You can be smart as long as you're not obviously smart. You know what I mean? Most men I've come in contact with might think, 'Yeah, she's smart.' But they never thought I was smarter than they were; sometimes they were underestimating me and sometimes they weren't. Sometimes I was a whole lot smarter than they were. But I was also smart enough not to have acted like I was smarter."

Viola Turner has an independent and creative spirit that she relates back to her parents. "They were very smart people. We had picnics all the time. As a matter of fact, I guess I had more parties than anybody in the whole world." Her father would take her to the Opera House and the City Auditorium for outstanding operas and minstrel shows. Her mother died when she was sixteen years old. However, her father continued to support the educational and career pursuits of his daughter.

Madie Hall Xuma

Madie Hall Xuma's passion and vocation was "to work for peace and justice, freedom and dignity for all people." Her personal motto was also the stated purpose of the YWCA. Madie Hall Xuma's lifework centered on this goal. She helped to create tremendous opportunities for women in the United States and in South Africa through the YWCA. She was an organizer and a leader. She served on the executive board for the YWCA's world organization for eight years. Her interest in the YWCA began in 1911 in North Carolina while she was a student at Shaw University in Raleigh. She also worked as a staff member of the YWCA in Lynchburg, Virginia, and later returned to her home of Winston-Salem to lay the groundwork for a YWCA for black girls and women. Her finest effort was in Johannesburg, South Africa, where, despite opposition from both the government and the white YWCA, she organized black women to form an organization. In Johannesburg, the YWCA was named the Zenzele YWCA, which means "people helping themselves" and celebrated its sixtieth anniversary in 2001.

At the center of Madie Hall Xuma's cosmopolitan life story were the influence of her parents and her relationship within her family, which contributed to her education and ambition. Her story begins in Winston-Salem, North Carolina, where Madie Hall was born in 1894 as one of four children of H. H. Hall and Ginny Cowan Hall. Her parents met in Salisbury, North Carolina, and attended Shaw University together. Dr. H. H. Hall graduated from Leonard Medical School at Shaw and married his schoolmate, Ginny. The young couple moved to Winston-Salem, where Dr. Hall was the first black physician in that city.

Dr. Hall arrived in Winston-Salem during a flu epidemic, and this turned out to be a critical time. "At first the white doctors wouldn't help him, in no way," Mrs. Xuma explained. However, because of the severity of the flu, "they were losing so many people, they would die like flies overnight. My father didn't lose a single patient. The black maid in the white homes would tell about this black doctor; they said, 'He's treating people, and he's not losing any. All his people are getting well.' And many of the whites began to flock to him, and the white doctors wanted to know what methods and medications he was using. He said, 'I learned it in school, and if you want to learn it, you'd better go back to school!'" Eventually, Dr. Hall organized the black medical community in Winston-Salem to plan for the city's first black hospital.

While she was a child, Madie Hall Xuma's father had an office in their home. She idolized her father and wanted to be just like him. "I was so fond of him carrying that black bag around. And I watched him and he would let me play around in his office. I was watching everything he did. I wanted to be a doctor, but he kept saying, 'No, no; no girl can be a doctor.'"

Nevertheless, Madie Hall Xuma describes her father as "the finest, sweetest, and kindest person I have ever known. And he was so in love with me, he just thought I was an angel from heaven. I was the first girl, and he did everything to make me happy. After my mother passed, we even got closer." From her father, she gained direction and support. He also instilled in her the importance of education and taking initiatives. From her mother, she developed a sense for business, organizational skills, and the value of giving to others who are less fortunate.

When Xuma graduated from Shaw University, she was accepted at the Howard University Medical School. Simultaneously, her brother was also accepted. However, Dr. Hall said that he would allow her brother (Leroy) to go, but she could not. Upon her inquiry as to why she could not go to medical school, Dr. Hall explained that he had one or two women in his medical class in 1890, and he had followed their careers after they went to work. They had a very hard time going out to treat patients in the country, traveling in the winter, and risking being molested. "He saw all of that happening to me if I became a physician. And he said, 'No, I'd rather you study anything but medicine.' I gave in and went into teaching. He was happy with that. My mother didn't oppose him. She just wanted me to get a college education."

After a year in Daytona, Florida, teaching and working with Mary McLeod Bethune, Madie Hall returned home upon her mother's death in 1930 to assume the responsibilities of the house and her mother's properties and to care for her father. "My father just handed everything over to me, and he went on about his business of practicing medicine. My mother trained me for dealing with household and business affairs. And I think she must have known it would fall on me one day."

After her father's death, Madie Hall traveled to New York and completed her parents' dream for her education. She completed her master's degree at Columbia University in 1937 at the age of forty-three. It was in New York that she met and later married Dr. Alfred B. Xuma of Johannesburg, South Africa. They resided in Johannesburg. Although she faced hostility initially from Africans and coloreds who were skeptical about the idea of Dr. Xuma marrying an American, she inevitably won the hearts of the people in the community—colored and white. Madie Hall Xuma and her husband rooted their lives in social service and activism, fighting for equal rights and against apartheid.

OCCUPATIONAL AND EDUCATIONAL ACHIEVEMENT: A COMPARATIVE ANALYSIS

All five women pursued professional occupations—two in education, one in social service administration, one in business administration, and one in publishing. The daughters included in this study worked before and during their marriages. Most of the daughters attained occupational ranks higher than those held by most of their mothers and husbands. Work for these women of achievement was a creative outlet as well as a source of income.

These women of achievement embraced leadership adventures. All left home to pursue college or graduate education. Three matriculated in schools located in the North, distant from their home communities in the South; three sought employment outside the area in which they grew up. Two experienced international travel—one to France for study at the Sorbonne and another to South Africa to marry a physician in Johannesburg and to establish YWCA centers there.

Although born in the closing years of the nineteenth century or the early years of the twentieth century, these women of achievement graduated from college and some continued their education with graduate studies. These were unusual accomplishments for women at that time. Some of these women were first-generation college students; others were not. In general, daughters attained educational levels similar to or often exceeding the educational accomplishments of their parents. All reached educational and professional levels equal to or exceeding those of their husbands.

These women of achievement may be described as pioneers as well as traditionalists. They were traditionalists in that, along the way, all participated in teaching as a career for various periods of time. Teaching was an occupation to which black women in the early part of the twentieth century could aspire. However, only two of these five women continued to teach during the entire course of their careers. The other three moved into traditionally male careers—business, publishing, and social service administration. They made significant contributions to society in these extraordinary occupational roles.

MENTORING: A COMPARATIVE ANALYSIS

Fathers in four of the five families in this study fulfilled the requirements of mentors. The daughters had enormous trust in their fathers and the fathers had great confidence in their daughters. Trust and confidence are the essence of an effective mentoring relationship. Turner said that her father was "dear" and "a sweet, loving man who gave her lots of attention," although he was the one father who did not advocate for his daughter's education. Xuma declared that her father supported her in every way, although he opposed her aspiration to be a physician largely because he thought such a profession would be hard and hazardous for his daughter. She called him "the finest and sweetest and the kindest person" that she had ever known. Her father loved her so much, she said, that he acted as if she was an "angel from heaven." He did everything to make her happy. Saunders said that she had an especially close relationship with her father. Saunders' father was proud of her and everything that she did. He was always on hand for any program in which his daughter participated and enveloped her with a feeling of confidence and protection.

Merrick designated herself as the carrier of a torch that was passed on to her by her father. Burnet, identifying completely with her father, said that she stood in his shoes and she credited him with giving her courage to face social issues directly. She still remembers and believes what her father repeatedly told her, that she is as good as anybody else. Although Merrick and Burnett attribute their missions to the concerns and influence of their fathers, clearly, these missions were not thrust upon resisting participants. Merrick promised to do everything she could do to keep her father's torch of service to others burning. To indicate how strongly she identified with the political activity of her father, Burnett said, "[I] stand in his shoes from the sole of his feet to the top of head."

Offspring identifying with the mission of their family, and particularly their father's public service activities, is not a new finding. What is new is the language these women use to describe their fathers. Three women described their fathers as loving, kind, dear, and supportive; the remaining two women said that the level of support received from their fathers was implicit in their relationships. These descriptions differ from the conclusion offered earlier by Jill Ker Conway, that fathers in black families are "uncertain quantities."

The fathers were proud of their daughters and had confidence in them. These are descriptors of relationships between protégés and mentors. The fathers were involved in many different activities with their children. Saunders' father was on hand for her college graduation when she delivered the senior oration. He was also present at other ceremonial occasions, even if her mother couldn't attend. Merrick's father took his two daughters on a cross-country train trip from North Carolina to California to attend the World's Fair; their mother stayed at home. Turner's father took his daughter to the opera house frequently to see live performances.

Even though Xuma's father did not endorse her ambition to be a physician, his action (from his point of view) was protective. Nonetheless, he valued education and supported her career in education and social service. Saunders said that her father always stood by her, especially in times of trouble. To walk beside him, she said, "was to feel confidence and his protective authority."

Four of the five fathers in these case studies performed the essential functions that qualified them as mentors. The only father not included in this number supported his daughter in many ways and acquiesced to his wife's judgment regarding the importance of education for their daughter. Three fathers enabled their daughters to fulfill occupational goals that were self-selected. Moreover, they gave their daughters a sense of security that enabled them to succeed because they were not afraid to risk failure.

9

The Myth of Black Matriarchy

By examining data that are controlled for race and social class, this analysis not only refutes categorically the myth of the black matriarchy but indicates that the equalitarian pattern of decision making appears to be the norm for American households, and that the cultural lag, if any, is found not among blacks but among middle-class white households that now are struggling toward the equalitarian goal.

The *American Journal of Sociology* published a study by Russell Middleton and Snell Putney that should have put to rest for all time the theory of the black matriarchy—the domineering woman in the black nuclear family (Middleton and Putney 1960: 605–609). Later, Delores Mack studied eighty couples and used methods similar to those in the Middleton and Putney study. Mack concluded that "marital dominance is not a trait but a context-dependent function of the relationship between two marriage partners" (Mack 1978: 148). Warren D. TenHouten studied 148 black families and 138 white families from higher and lower socioeconomic levels and concluded that most of the families were egalitarian (TenHouten 1970: 145–173). In 1983, Willie reported that his studies of black families in working-class and middle-class status levels "confirm the presence of equalitarian decision making and reject the notion of matriarchal or female-dominated households" (Willie 1983: 159). In the year 2000, Bart Landry found that "[t]he broader definition of womanhood championed by black middle-class women struck a blow for an expansion of women's rights in society and a more egalitarian position in the home, making for a far more progressive system among blacks at this time than among whites" (Landry 2000: 81).

Robert Staples (1970) and Jacquelyne Johnson Jackson (1973) have called "the black matriarchy" a myth. Jackson stated that even with the presence of evidence against it, some white social scientists continue to write about "black female dominance over black society" (Jackson 1973: 186–199). The purpose of this discussion is twofold: (1) to examine patterns of dominance in black and white families by social class and (2) to speculate on the reasons why some social scientists continue to ignore these findings.

Many studies about the effect of race upon various forms of behavior are not comparative. Interpretations about race and race-related events are likely to be erroneous when limited to examination of only one racial population. Even when comparative studies are undertaken, social scientists must guard against the In-group/Out-group Syndrome—the tendency to study the positive adaptations in the racial population with which one identifies and the negative adaptations in the other groups.

Fortunately, Middleton and Putney steered clear of this syndrome. For this reason, it should be of value to reexamine their data. These two social scientists analyzed the decision-making experience in nuclear families, while controlling for social class and race. Despite the small size of the sample, the careful way in which Middleton and Putney designed their study and the absence of biased assumptions cause this to be a valuable investigation into the association, if any, among race, socioeconomic status, and authority practices within the family.

A reexamination of the Middleton and Putney data provides an opportunity to confirm or cast doubt on the presence of a matriarchy not only in black families but also in white families. Essentially this is the reason for a reexamination of these data. Our concern is with determining the dominance pattern, if any, in family decision making in black and in white racial populations. A comparative analysis is of value in determining the relative effect of race and social class.

Specifically, forty families were studied—twenty black and twenty white. Each racial study group was divided equally between white-collar and blue-collar workers. Ten college professors were selected in a random way to represent the black middle class, and ten tradesmen were randomly selected to represent the black working class. A similar procedure was followed in obtaining a white sample included in the study. The spouses were American-born, had been married two or more years, were twenty to forty-nine years of age, had at least one child, and all resided in the same small town.

A fifteen-item questionnaire was filled out separately by each spouse in a household. Later the spouses conferred and then filled out the same questionnaire jointly. Questions had to do with childcare, family purchasing activity, decisions about standard-of-living, recreation, and role relationships. An example of the questions is the following: "If you were buying a house, would you prefer to buy a small new house or a large but older house costing the same amount?" When filling out the questionnaire jointly, the couple was asked to arrive at a family decision if answers for each spouse were not the same. If the husband won two-third or more of the "joint decisions"—that is, if the wife changed her answer to that indicated by the husband—then the dominance pattern for the family was classified as patriarchal. If the wife won two-thirds or more of the "joint decisions," the family was labeled matriarchal. An equalitarian family was one in which there was a considerable amount of give and take in decision making, so that one spouse prevailed less than two-thirds and the other more than one-third of the times when they differed with respect to decisions about a family activity.

The most outstanding finding is that middle-class and working-class black families tend to be equalitarian. Seventeen of the twenty black households in this study made joint decisions in which the husband tended to win about as often as the wife when there was a difference of opinion between them. Among blacks, the middle class was the most equalitarian; nine out of ten of these families resolved their differences with neither the husband nor the wife always dominating. Of the three black families out of the twenty that were not equalitarian, two in the working class were matriarchal and one in the middle class was patriarchal. In terms of this analysis, 85 percent of nuclear families among middle-class and working-class blacks are equalitarian in household decision making. The myth of the black matriarchy—the domineering wife—is refuted by these data.

This experience of equalitarian decision making in black households differed sharply from what was observed among whites. Most white families were equalitarian too. But the proportion was down to 65 percent, or thirteen out of the twenty nuclear white families in the study. Of the seven white families out of twenty that were not equalitarian, four were matriarchal (two in the middle class and two in the working class) and three were patriarchal (two in the middle class and one in the working class).

Among whites, the most outstanding finding had to do with the middle class. There was equalitarian agreement in family decision making at this social-class level in only six of the ten households. The other four were dominated in decision making either by the husband or the wife. This tug-of-war between spouses in many middle-class white households clearly differed from the decision-making experience in middle-class black households, where nine out of ten were classed as equalitarian.

Although nuclear white families were moving toward the goal of an equalitarian pattern of decision making, they had residuals of both matriarchal and patriarchal dominance. Competition between these two forms of decision making was most pronounced among middle-class whites. The strong identification of male and female role responsibilities in some middle-class white households is an example of the absence of a universal equalitarian experience. White women in this class category tend to dominate in childcare decisions, and white men tend to prevail in decisions regarding the standard of living and household purchases. This separation in role behavior and household responsibility for husband and wife is more rigid in middle-class nuclear white families than in any other race-class group.

THE MACK STUDY

Delores Mack (1978) studied eighty couples in their homes to determine whether their relationships were matriarchal, patriarchal, or equalitarian. Her methods were similar to those in the Middleton and Putney study. Twenty couples from each of the following race-class categories were included in the study: black middle class, white middle class, black working class, white working class. She administered a questionnaire to each of the spouses separately. Then the spouses were asked to complete another copy of the questionnaire jointly. White husbands and black husbands were found to be similar in the amount of decision-making power they wielded in this exercise. There was a statistically significant difference in the power of husbands, according to social class, with working-class husbands having more power than middle-class husbands.

Delores Mack asked the couples to participate in three additional tasks. The spouses were asked to discuss two specific issues for five minutes each. Then discussions were analyzed according to the percentage of time the husbands spoke. There were no differences on this measure by race or by class. In a bargaining task in which the husband played a salesperson and the wife a customer, middle-class husbands were able to obtain a higher selling price from their wives than were working-class husbands, but there were no differences by race. Finally, each spouse was asked to rate who the dominant partner was in the marriage. Husbands tended to perceive themselves as only slightly more dominant than their wives, and there were no racial or social class differences. All the wives saw their husbands as slightly more dominant than themselves, although black working-class wives perceived themselves as the most dominant.

Mack points out that "marital dominance is not a trait but a context-dependent function of the relationship between two marriage partners" (Mack 1978: 148).

THE TENHOUTEN STUDY

Another study utilized interview data from a large number of families. Ten-Houten (1970) interviewed 148 black families and 138 white families from both the higher and lower socioeconomic status rankings. Husbands and wives were asked to respond to nine items comprising a "male dominance ideology scale." Blacks were significantly higher on male dominance than whites for each of the nine items. Those from the lower socioeconomic group were higher on male dominance than those from the higher socioeconomic group. The group with the highest male dominance ideology was the black lower socioeconomic group.

When TenHouten asked children to rank their parents in terms of who dominates the decision-making process, he found that white lower socioeconomic families were mostly likely to be husband-dominated, while the other three groups were most likely to be autonomous or equalitarian. Spouses were asked if mothers should dominate parental roles. Members of the lower socioeconomic group agreed that mothers should dominate this process, although response did not vary by race.

On the basis of these findings, TenHouten concludes that there is no support for Moynihan's (1965) thesis that lower socioeconomic black families are matriarchies. At least one of his measures indicates that fathers in the black lower socioeconomic group have more power than those in the other four groups.

Earlier in this book, we discovered that "middle-class status for most black families is a result of dual employment of husband and wife" and that "the economic foundation for most middle-class black families is a product of the cooperative work of husband and wife." One could call their way of life, "a genuine team effort." In these family studies conducted in the 1970s, Willie found that "few, if any, family functions including cooking, cleaning, and shopping are considered to be the exclusive prerogative of the husband or wife." Based on these findings, we called black women in the middle-class family, "the best example of [a] liberated wife in American society" because "she and her husband have acted as partners out of necessity and, thus, have carved out an equalitarian pattern of interaction in which neither husband nor wife has ultimate authority" (Willie 1976: 19–23).

Bart Landry, one of the nation's leading scholars on black family life (particularly black middle-class families), has made an observation similar to that seen by others. He said that "in the course of their activities for racial uplift, . . . [black] wives developed and promoted their own unique conception of true womanhood[,] . . . a conception that united rather than separated the public and private sphere, a conception that championed a wider role for married women than domesticity. It argued for equality in marriage and valued employment as the key to achieving equality in marriage and society as well as to fulfilling lives for themselves" (Landry 2000: 31).

Among the black working class, we found that "family life . . . is a struggle for survival which requires the cooperative effort of all—husband, wife, and children." We found that "the cohesion of the black working-class family results not so much from understanding and tenderness shown by one for the other as from the joint and heroic effort to stave off adversity. Without the income of either parent or the contributions of children from part-time employment, the family would topple back into poverty." Household chores have to be shared because husbands and wives sometimes are engaged in what has been described as "tandem parenting." For example, "In some households, the husband works during the daytime and the wife during the evening hours. Such work schedules mean that the family as a unit is not able to share any meals together." We found that despite these and other hardships, "There is a constancy among the members of the black working-class families which tends to pull them together." The black working-class husband or wife knows that "his or her destiny is dependent upon the actions of the other." While there is a tendency for the spouses to have assigned roles, "in time of crisis, these roles can change;" and crisis is a perennial in working-class black families. Thus, there is a good deal of role exchange between family members, including older children who may take on some parental responsibilities of socializing younger members of the household. To sum up, one could say that "almost everything which the black working-class parents do to achieve success and respectability is extraordinary. . . . Their education is limited; their occupations are unskilled; their income is modest; and their families are relatively large. Yet they dream the impossible dreams about doing for their children what they could not do for themselves. By hook or crook, they—the parents—manage to do it when others said it couldn't be done" (Willie 1976: 59–64, 94).

Black wives have worked as members of the labor force during their marriages. A higher proportion of black married women compared to white married women are in the labor force. But black women tend to earn less money than white working women. Indeed, black women are doubly discriminated against. They earn less money than white women and they tend to earn less money than black men. Nevertheless, they persevere. These families that stay together through thick and thin and in richer or poorer circumstances have taught this society something about commitment, as well as something about loyalty and something about love.

In our judgment, one of the greatest gifts of blacks to the culture of the nation has been the egalitarian family model in which neither the husband nor the wife is always in charge. This is a family model in which husbands and wives work, pool their money, and make ultimate sacrifices for their children so that they may have a more abundant life than the older generation. In the black egalitarian family, men are not always the head and the supreme power, and women are not always weak and dependent. It would be wise for others to observe the egalitarian family as a model of mutual empowerment and mutual fulfillment.

This analysis does more than call into question the myth of the black matriarchy; it indicates that the tendency, if any, toward a matriarchy (or wife dominance in household decision making in American society) is most visible among whites, especially in the middle-class nuclear white family. It is not the purpose of this analysis to contribute to a new myth of the white matriarchy while disposing of an old myth about the black matriarchy. Clearly equalitarian decision making is the prevailing practice among white as well as black families. Among whites, however, this practice is under attack by residual practices of matriarchal and patriarchal dominance.

These residual practices give a clue as to why some social scientists, as charged by Jackson, continue to make assertions about the black matriarchy. Possibly they are projecting upon blacks their own experience of households dominated by females. The act of projecting, of believing others have thoughts, feelings, and experiences similar to our own, is probably one of the greatest impediments to the development of valid social science knowledge and understandings. The distorting effects of projecting occur most frequently among those social scientists who believe that any behavior of blacks that is not imitative of whites is deviant. It is appropriate to conjecture, on the basis of facts presented in this analysis, that Daniel P. Moynihan's statement that "the Negro community has been forced into a matriarchal structure" is a form of projection upon blacks of what he had seen among whites (U.S. Department of Labor 1965: 29). Rather than blacks being modeled in the image of whites, as Moynihan suggested they should be, to facilitate their progress, the evidence indicates that white families are moving in the direction of equalitarian decision making that has characterized most black households.

The process of projecting has caused other social scientists to perpetrate the same error that Moynihan committed. Howard Taylor said that "Jencks . . . takes considerable liberties in discussing the effects of integration, segregation, race, etc., upon occupational and income equality." According to Taylor, Jencks "clearly infers that education is not related to success for black people; that if blacks want more money, then more education will not get it." Then Taylor introduced a surprising piece of evidence against Jencks. He said that inferences by Jencks were based on a statistical technique called path analysis, and that data used in the analysis were obtained from "native white nonfarm males who took an armed forces IQ test!" Taylor discovered that "not one single path analysis in the entire report is performed on even one black sample." The fallacy of "studying whites and then generalizing to blacks without studying blacks directly is consistently made in 'important' social science research documents," according to Taylor (Taylor 1977: 245–246).

Overcoming the fallacy of projecting will encourage social scientists to study all racial populations directly and to learn from them the beneficial and harmful effects of various patterns of adaptation. By examining data that are controlled for race and social class, this analysis not only refuted categorically the myth of the black matriarchy but also indicated that the equalitarian pattern of decision making appears to be the norm for American households.

IV

BLACK FAMILIES AND THE
SOCIAL SYSTEM

10

The Case for the Black Male

The black male is a difficult topic to discuss, so much misinformation has been written about him. The case against the black male is being prosecuted in the mass media with white public opinion serving as both judge and jury, and some blacks participating as accusatory expert witnesses. What is strange about this trial is that the accused is not permitted to defend himself. The mass media tend to ignore information that could exonerate the accused.

The *Boston Globe* published an article on black men and black women a few years ago (Reynolds 1985: B23, B26). It was entitled "Black Men-Black Women: The Expectation Gap." Despite its title, the article really was an assault on the character of black men. Then Bill Moyers trotted out his CBS documentary on "The Vanishing Family—A Crisis in Black America," which highlighted Timothy, an unmarried black father of many children whom columnist George Will called a "paradigm" of guiltless sexual irresponsibility. George Will said, "The Timothys are more of a menace to black progress than the Bull Connors were" (Will 1986: 11).

Alice Walker's prize-winning book, *The Color Purple*, made its debut in 1982. Now a major motion picture, the book, said *Essence* magazine, reveals truth about black men and black women, and the *New York Review of Books* said that Alice Walker called into being a whole submerged world. As you may know, the book begins with a letter to God written by a fourteen-year-old black girl who tells how she was raped by her stepfather (Walker 1982: 1). From this point on, the Alice Walker story about black men gets uglier and uglier and becomes, in effect, a stereotype of some poor black men as well as a manifestation of self-hatred among some black women.

Why is maladaptive behavior among black individuals classified as a paradigm or model? When such behavior is found among whites, why is it not generalized and referred to as a paradigm or model? As a paradigm or model, maladaptive behavior allegedly impacts an entire population group.

In his 1965 report on *The Negro Family*, Daniel Moynihan said, "The white family, despite many variants, remains a powerful agency" (U.S. Department of Labor 1965: 35). Sociologically, the same may be said of the black family. But neither Will nor Moynihan came to this conclusion. Moynihan declared that "White children without fathers at least perceive all about them the pattern of men working" (U.S. Department of Labor 1965: 35). However, without producing comparative evidence, Moynihan concluded that "Negro children without fathers flounder and fail" (U.S. Department of Labor 1965: 35). The inference is that white children without fathers do not flounder and fail. A recent report on poor white families in South Boston reveals information that is contrary to the Moynihan conclusion (MacDonald 1999).

The stereotype that there is no pathology among poor whites must be corrected. Writer Ken Auletta has provided a firsthand account of life in Preston County, West Virginia, in the Appalachian area. Preston County is rural and predominantly white. Thirty-one percent of the population is classified as poor. This is three times the proportion of whites in the nation so classified. Nearly 70 percent of the residents have lived in the same house all of their lives, so their poverty is a persistent phenomenon (Auletta 1982: 159).

In terms of personal characteristics, poor white men in this county have an average of less than nine years of schooling. The average mother in Preston County receives welfare and has received it more than six years. Auletta called welfare "a way of life" among these people. Being poor is no social stigma in Preston County (Auletta 1982: 160). Incest is common, too, and family troubles haunt the poor white people of Preston County. Auletta said, "alcohol, unemployment, . . . frustration, and boredom generate violence in the home," of which women are often the victims (Auletta 1982: 160).

Carolyn Chute's novel, *The Beans of Egypt, Maine*, is also about the way of life of the white poor. The opening pages in Carolyn Chutes' story about poor whites are not much different from the opening pages of Alice Walker's story about poor blacks.

In both novels, the mother is ill and the man in the house turns to a daughter in the house for sexual favors. In *The Beans of Egypt, Maine*, the white daughter sleeps in bed with her daddy, not just in the afternoon when her daddy has a pain in his back and has to take a nap but also at nighttime, too, according to the book (Chute 1985:1–3). And the stepfather forces sexual intercourse upon his black stepdaughter in *The Color Purple* (Walker 1982: 1). There are babies in and out of wedlock and plenty of fussing and fighting in the white households of the poor in rural Maine, according to Chute, and in the black households of the poor in rural Alabama, according to Walker.

The Beans of Egypt, Maine and *The Color Purple* reveal similarities between poor blacks and poor whites. Actually the portraits of the black poor and especially poor black men contained in the *Boston Globe* article and in the CBS documentary are similar to descriptions of poor white men in social science literature as well as in novels. In Willie's study of *Black and White Families*, the literature regarding what is known about poor white families is summarized (Willie 1985). Poor white men are as likely to project their frustrations upon poor white women by way of violent behavior as are the poor in any other population. This conversation was recorded between a police officer and a poor white man who is identified as a hillbilly:

> Police officer: "Look, you've got four kids. What if they found out you beat up their mother? Why did you do it?"
> Hillbilly: "She got out of line and I stomped her."
> Police officer: "What would you have done if your father had done it to your mother?"
> Hillbilly: "He did it all the time" (Auletta 1982: 160).

Thomas Cottle reports a similar experience of family violence among whites. This interview is with a twelve-year-old son:

> The son: "You know what I've been doing for six months? I've been a referee for all their fights?"
> Interviewer: "Your parents have been fighting?"
> The son: "Just about every night."
> Interviewer: "Your dad?"
> The son: "Mother, too. Both of them. Screaming, hitting. Breaking furniture. They're all right for two or three nights, then they're back at it."
> Interviewer: "What started it?"
> The son: "I don't know. One night, I think maybe it was New Years' Eve, I was in bed and they were fighting. Dad pushed her or hit her and she fell. I waited for a while and then went in. She had this big cut over her eye. I had to push Dad away. Another night I carried Mom into my bedroom. She was barely conscious. Then another night she must have hit him pretty hard because when I got in there his nose was bleeding. It wasn't broken, but he was crying and she was crying."
> The son: "Dad gets awful angry, you know."
> Interviewer: "I didn't know."
> The son: "Well, he can. I never saw him hurt anyone, but he's always picked on Mom" (Cottle 1975: 7–8).

The interesting thing about this report in family pathology is that the family is not poor, but the family is white. The father is an automotive executive and has a more than adequate income. Despite the novels, newspaper articles, and television documentaries about poor blacks, comparative social science data indicate that pathology and maladaptive behavior are not limited to poor black men. Indeed, maladaptive behavior is not limited to any racial group or social class category. Whites and blacks of all class levels have their share of pathology and so do the affluent and the poor.

The *Boston Globe* article carried this subheadline: "Black Men Are Falling Behind Black Women." *Essence* magazine editor, Susan Taylor, said that headlines like this one are a myth because black women are on the bottom of the ladder, economically. "They make 92 cents for every $1.00 a black man makes," she said. While *Essence* has published articles on the stresses of black male-black female relationships, Editor Susan Taylor said, "The reality is that there is a war on black people in America," and that neither black men nor black women should "buy into the myth" that one or the other is enjoying some kind of privilege. Taylor concluded that the myth has been cultivated as a way to further pit black man and women against each other (Reynolds 1985: B23, B25).

The *Boston Globe* included Susan Taylor's contradicting testimony in its case against the black male, as a good newspaper should, but then immediately ignored the wisdom of her remarks. The reporter continued to build the case against black men. To counter Susan Taylor's statements, the report introduced expert opinion from a few blacks with intimate knowledge of black ghetto and slum life. The first witness was a black lawyer, the president of Boston Black Men's Association. He said that black youngsters have no positive black male role models and black boys do not have any goals other than possibly achieving as athletes and musicians. Another witness quoted was a fourteen-year-old black male resident of Roxbury. He said that many of his friends had dropped out of school but that they probably would have remained in school if they had a father living with them. These statements described black boys as failures and suggested that black men were contributing to their failure.

Moreover, black boys were described as not aspiring to attend college, never dreaming of becoming a professor or politician, and not thinking about a career as a doctor, lawyer, or businessman. Rather, they were characterized as having high rates of unemployment, crime, and incarceration. In summary, black males were portrayed as hanging around the street and getting into trouble. Their problems were described by the *Boston Globe*'s reporter as leading to an unbroken cycle of poverty and little upward social mobility.

Mothers were ignored, dismissed, or denied as being of any consequence in the lives of their black sons by the *Boston Globe* reporter. Black wives of black husbands were completely ignored in the article. It was asserted that black boys turn more to their peers for support and direction than to their mothers.

Studies about middle-class black families that we recently reviewed came to conclusions that are opposite to those that were offered to the *Boston*

Globe reporter. Annie Barnes said, "studies of black families have primarily focused on the low-income and working-class communities." These studies, she said, have emphasized matrifocality, a concept that describes domestic units dominated by females. Annie Barnes said, "This is a type of family found among [some] lower-class families in which [the man in the house] appears to be unsuited for steady employment" (Barnes 1983: 55). The error in most studies of black families, Barnes asserts, is "the phenomenon of lumping all blacks together and sometimes comparing them with the white middle class" (Barnes 1983: 56).

Barnes studied middle-class black families in Atlanta, Georgia, and found circumstances quite different from those described by the *Boston Globe*. She found that a majority of the black men and women in her study had attended college; a higher proportion of black women than black men had graduated from college and gone on to graduate school. But a higher proportion of black men compared to black women had obtained doctoral degrees. She also found that a majority of both middle-class black men and middle-class black women held white-collar jobs but that black women outnumbered black men in these jobs by twelve percentage points. Barnes classified some of the black middle-class families in Atlanta as matriarchal, but they were a minority of the middle-class black families that she studied (Barnes 1983: 60).

Walter Allen studied a sample of middle-class blacks in Chicago. About one-third of the black men and slightly more than one-fourth of the black women in his study had attended college (Allen 1983: 80). About half of the black men and slightly more than one-quarter of the women held white-collar jobs (Allen 1983: 81). For the most part, Allen discovered that the black wives in middle-class black families reported greater marital satisfaction than their husbands (Allen 1983: 83). Race, however, had little to do with variation in marital adjustment according to Allen (Allen 1983: 85).

Finally, Donald Addison reported the results of his study of black middle-class wives in Crescent City, Iowa. In Addison's study, the women found their men to be temperate, industrious, faithful, and trustworthy (Addison 1983: 98–99). Addison said that while the literature on black family life tends to characterize black men as "weak, unprincipled individuals with minimum concern for [their] family" (Addison 1983: 100), the black women in his study characterized husbands as "faithful and emotionally strong" (Addison 1983: 109).

One might object to the fact that studies cited have been of middle-class black families only. The *Boston Globe* reporter wrote about poor black families only. If the way of life of middle-class black men is not representative of all blacks, neither is the way of life of poor black men representative of all blacks. Yet, the reporter presented the troubles of some poor black men and their relationships with some poor black women as if they were indicative of the relationship between all black men and black women. Only one-fourth of the black population is below the poverty line. Thus, stories about poor blacks discuss a minority sector of the black population in the United States.

The mass media commentators and reporters who assert that poor black boys have no male role models, pay little attention to what their mothers say or do, believe they can earn money and be upwardly mobile through professional athletics and music only, and never dream of becoming a professor, politician, doctor, or lawyer, make assertions that are contrary to some of the findings reported in this volume.

Actually, black men along with black women, as stated earlier, have contributed to a revolutionary practice in family relations in this nation. The source of this practice, like other good things blacks contribute, has remained invisible or been ignored. The revolution which black men and women have created by rejecting the Moynihan sexist notion of perpetual male leadership is the equalitarian family in which neither partner always prevails. Walter Allen reported that satisfaction ratings increase in families in which power is shared and decrease in authoritarian structures—patriarchal or matriarchal (Allen 1983: 77). The equalitarian black family is a manifestation of this principal and its way of life could benefit all. Therefore, we assert that black men with the help of black women are revolutionizing the power relationship between men and women in the kinship system (Willie 1981). This new relationship and arrangement is the prevailing pattern now in all U.S. households, with whites following the lead of blacks. Public opinion specialist Louis Harris found that "a majority of married people are convinced that marriage is no longer an arrangement whereby the husband assumes the breadwinning responsibilities and the wife takes over the household management and childrearing. To the contrary, both men and women are now convinced that a marriage in which both husband and wife work and share the housekeeping and child care is a better one" (Harris 1987: 129).

Black parents in the past have insisted that their daughters receive an education similar to or better than that provided for their sons as a way of overcoming the discriminatory effects of sexism against women. And black husbands in general have encouraged black wives to enter the labor force and to pursue occupations that sometimes are more prestigious than their own. If measures of satisfaction in marriage grow with the increasing experience of equalitarianism, then this new style of social relations that does not presume male leadership in private and public affairs is something of value to which the rest of society is and should be exploring. Blessed by black men and women who have kept alive the belief in equality in household and other human affairs, our nation has not recognized equalitarianism in the family as a major contribution to social life in this nation that emerged from the black experience. It has not recognized this because it has been too busy damning black males.

This bit of moral alchemy in which the good things that black males do are transformed into bad things is not new. One of the worse names to attach to a black male is to call him Uncle Tom. Unfortunately, many, including some blacks, have not read Harriet Beecher Stowe's book, *Uncle Tom's Cabin*. It was Tom who sacrificed his freedom so that his master could raise enough money from the sale of his faithful servant to pay off debts and keep the plantation and the other slaves who were Tom's family and friends together until emancipation. No other slave sale could have brought as much money as the sale of Tom. If Tom had escaped to the freedom that was his eternal ambition, debtors would have foreclosed on his master and sold all of the slaves "down the river" to owners who were more inclined to brutalize them. Tom knew this and sacrificed his freedom so that the slave community of which he had been a part could remain together under the protection of a benign rather than a brutal owner.

Tom never made it back to the plantation of his original master as he hoped he would. He died standing up to Legree, the most hated slave owner in the South. Tom was ordered to whip a woman slave. Tom replied, "I beg Mas'r's pardon. . . . It's what I ain't used to,—never did,—and can't do, no way possible." Then he said, "This yer thing I can't feel it right to do;—and, Mas'r, I never shall do it,—never!" Finally, Tom said, "Mas'r, if you mean to kill me, kill me; but, as to my raising my hand agin any one here, I n'ver shall—any one here, I'll die first!" And die, Tom did. A sacrificial death, he died. While the tears and blood flowed down his face, said Harriet Beecher Stowe, Tom exclaimed, "No! no! my soul an't yours, Mas'r! You haven't bought it,—Ye can't buy it!" (Stowe 1852: 364–366). Tom understood sacrifice and suffering for the sake of others. His is a marvelous legacy not unlike that of Jesus Christ, Moses, Gandhi, and Martin Luther King Jr.

How is it that the name of a black man who perfected the practice of sacrificial love has become an appellation of disdain? Sociologist Robert K. Merton said that the moral alchemist transforms what is a virtue for the in-group into a vice when found among the out-group (Merton 1949). So sacrificial love, which is good when found among white men, is bad when exhibited among black men, according to some mass media reporters. Thus, acting with courage and sacrifice, which are virtues when found among whites, is transformed into a vice when exhibited among blacks such as Uncle Tom. People who participate in such racial transformations are appropriately labeled moral alchemists. Black men and women should be honored for discovering and refining the equalitarian family form. Instead they are ridiculed if their families do not act like white families.

There is something strange and even demonic about the case against the black male. Maybe the origin of this strange, demonic behavior is as ancient as the story of the birth of Jesus in an oppressed Jewish family. The Jewish mother, Mary, has been venerated. But the Jewish father, Joseph, has been virtually ignored. And yet it was an act of acceptance and grace for Joseph to accept his wife and care for her child even though he was told that he was not the father. Mary did not earn the right to be the mother of Jesus. But, according to the law of that time, Joseph had the right to divorce a wife who was with child allegedly not his own. Joseph did not respond according to the law. He, a poor and persecuted Jewish man, responded according to the requirements of grace. And for so doing, Joseph has become invisible and virtually ignored when the story of the birth of Jesus is celebrated annually. Black men, and especially poor black men, exist in the tradition of Joseph— invisible, ignored, and denied. Nevertheless, their way of life is something of value—essential and significant in social organization. The lessons they can teach we ignore at our peril.

11

Socioeconomic Status among Racial Groups

If education, occupation, and income are used as archetype variables to examine the continuing significance of race, several interesting findings are revealed.

We agree with the assessment of the U.S. Department of Education contained in the year 2000 edition of *Digest of Educational Statistics*: "Americans have become more educated. In 1999, 83 percent of the population twenty-five years old and over had completed high school and 25 percent [of the people in this age range] had completed four or more years of college. . . . About 6 percent held a master's degree as their highest degree, slightly more than 1 percent held a professional degree (e.g. medicine or law), and 1 percent held a doctor's degree" (U.S. Department of Education 2000: 6, 18). These high achievement levels have been attained by citizens in all racial groups. For example, in 1999, more than three-quarters of black people twenty-five years old and over had graduated from high school; 41 percent had attended college; and 16 percent had graduated from college with a bachelor's degree, a few earning master's or doctorate degrees (U.S. Department of Education 2000: 18).

The better-educated population in this nation tends to be engaged in work that is intrinsically interesting. By the year 2000, 80.3 percent of the population twenty-five to sixty-four years of age was in the labor force. The opportunity to work, also, was distributed among all racial groups. For example, 80.8 percent of white people and 77.9 percent of black people in this age range participated in the labor force (U.S. Census Bureau 2001: 369).

The first and fundamental fact about black contemporary family life is the increasing socioeconomic differentiation found among such households in the United States. This is a fact that should be celebrated. E. Franklin Frazier reported in an article published near the midpoint of the twentieth century that only approximately one-eighth of black families were able to maintain a middle-class way of life (in Edwards 1968: 207). Studies of black families during the 1970s by Charles V. Willie revealed that about one-fourth had an annual income at or above the national median. Our research supports this trend in the findings for the 1990s, with one-third of household incomes at or above the national median in black families (U.S. Census Bureau 2001: 433). Growing affluence is a fact of life within the black population that has been recognized by a range of scholars, including William Wilson (1978) and Reynolds Farley and Walter Allen (1987).

In income, occupational opportunity, and educational attainment, Farley reports definite improvement among black households. The gap in median school year completed between black and white groups has been substantially reduced; the proportion of blacks in prestigious and higher-paying jobs has increased, as seen in the tables of data presented in this chapter. Reynolds Farley reports that "while blacks still have . . . high poverty and unemployment rates as compared with whites, opportunities for recent generations are much improved and, in all major metropolises, there are now moderate to large middle-class black populations" (Farley 1995: xi).

Some social scientists such as Wilson assert that race-specific policies to ameliorate the problems of poor blacks have disproportionately profited more advantaged black families. In effect, he links "the improving position of the black middle-class" to "the worsening condition of the black underclass" (Wilson 1987: ix, vii). The Wilson analysis is flawed on two counts: it does not demonstrate that poverty among blacks is increasing, and it does not provide a logical explanation of how help for one sector of the black population is harmful to another.

We know from an analysis of data published by the U.S. Bureau of the Census over the years that the proportion of black and white families below the poverty line has been reduced. In 1959, approximately 56 percent of all blacks lived below the poverty level. Today, the proportion is one-fourth. In 1959, about 18.1 percent of all whites lived below the poverty line; today, this proportion is about 10 percent (U.S. Census Bureau, 2001: 442). The proportion of black poor was 3.4 times greater than the proportion of white poor in 1959, and is 2.4 times greater today. While there has been progress, there is still a sizable proportional gap among the races (U.S. Census Bureau 2001: 442).

Missing from most analyses of black family life are positive adaptations and contributions to American society by blacks. Moreover, many studies of black family life stereotype blacks as if all were poor. Finally, some studies do not link descriptive findings to any theoretical framework that facilitates an explanation of the data. The assessment of black families reported here attempts to overcome these problems. A ratio of the proportion of black families with incomes in the lowest quintile of the range in 1954 was 2.17 times greater than the proportion of whites similarly situated. However, in 1999, forty-five years later, the ratio of the proportions for these two populations was down to 1.72. In the highest quintile of family income, the proportions of blacks at this income level was only .27 of that for whites in 1954. By 1999, the ratio of the proportion of blacks to whites in the highest fifth had almost doubled to .48. The actual proportion of blacks and other races in the bottom fifth of the family income hierarchy decreased from 43.3 percent in 1954 to 31 percent in 1999; in the top fifth of the family income hierarchy, the proportion of blacks and other races increased from 5.3 percent to 10.1 percent in 1999 (http://ferret.bls.census.gov/macro/032001/jjinc/new06_001.htm).

This analysis indicates the importance of studying the prevalence rate of families by race for the entire range of income categories rather than focusing only on measures of central tendency such as the mean, median, or mode. This analysis reveals that race continues as a significant variable differentiating blacks from whites at most income levels, and that the proportion of poor black families has decreased while the proportion of affluent black families has increased. At the close of the 1970s, for example, the proportion of professional and managerial workers among white males (30.5 percent) was nearly twice as great as the proportion of such workers employed as laborers and service workers (15.9 percent). The converse was true for black males: their proportion of laborers and service workers (31.4 percent) was nearly twice as great as the proportion of black professional and managerial workers (17.4 percent). Nevertheless, there was a change for blacks both at the top and the bottom of the occupational hierarchy. The modest increase in the proportion of blacks who got high-income jobs during the 1970s was accompanied by a modest decrease in black workers in low-income jobs. Later in this chapter we will revisit these occupational statistics to determine changes, if any, in occupational opportunities since the 1970s.

Education may be conceptualized as an input variable, occupation as a process variable, and income as an output variable. If these three are interrelated, then what one earns is a function of the kind of work one performs. And the kind of work one performs is based on educational attainment. High-level education as an input variable should beget high-level employment as a process variable and high-level income as an outcome variable.

In 1970, the median income for black households (in 1999 constant dollars) was $22,336, compared to a median of $36,696 for white households. The median for blacks was only 61 percent of that for whites. By 1999, the median for black households (in 1999 constant dollars) had increased by $5,574 to $27,910. However, the median income for white households also increased to $42,504. Despite an increase in black household incomes during this period of time, the median for blacks (in 1999 constant dollars) continued to lag behind that for white households, and, in 1999, was only 66 percent of the median for whites. This increase, of course, represented progress for blacks, but a very modest rate of relative progress, as seen in table 11.1 (U.S. Census Bureau 2001: 433).

Table 11.1. Money Income of Households—Percent Distribution by Income Level, Race, and Hispanic Origin, in Constant (1999) Dollars: 1970 to 1999 [Constant dollars based on CPI-U deflator. Households as of March of following year. Based on Current Population Survey; see text, Sections 1 and 13, and Appendix III.]

Year	Number of Households (1,000)	Percent Distribution								Median Income (Dollars)
		Under $10,000	$10,000– $14,999	$15,000– $24,999	$25,000– $34,999	$35,000– $49,999	$50,000– $74,999	$75,000 and Over		

Year	Number of House-holds (1,000)	Under $10,000	$10,000– $14,999	$15,000– $24,999	$25,000– $34,999	$35,000– $49,999	$50,000– $74,999	$75,000 and Over	Median Income (Dollars)
ALL HOUSEHOLDS[1]									
1970	64,778	12.9	7.4	14.5	15.2	21.2	18.7	10.1	35,232
1980	82,368	11.6	8.2	15.3	13.9	18.4	19.4	13.1	35,851
1985	88,458	11.8	7.8	15.1	13.6	17.6	18.4	15.8	36,568
1990	94,312	11.0	7.4	14.3	13.7	17.5	18.5	17.6	38,168
1995	99,627	10.8	8.0	15.0	13.6	16.6	18.0	17.9	37,251
1996	101,018	11.0	8.1	14.6	13.4	16.1	18.3	18.5	37,686
1997	102,528	10.6	7.8	14.6	12.9	16.3	18.3	19.7	38,411
1998	103,874	10.1	7.6	13.8	13.1	15.8	18.7	20.9	39,744
1999	104,705	9.2	7.3	14.1	12.7	15.8	18.4	22.6	40,816
WHITE									
1970	57,575	11.7	6.9	13.9	15.1	21.9	19.7	10.9	36,696
1980	71,872	10.1	7.6	14.9	14.0	18.9	20.5	14.1	37,822
1985	76,576	10.1	7.4	14.6	13.7	18.0	19.3	16.9	38,565
1990	80,968	9.2	7.0	14.1	13.8	17.9	19.3	18.7	39,809
1995	84,511	9.3	7.6	14.7	13.6	16.9	18.7	19.1	39,099
1996	85,059	9.3	7.7	14.4	13.4	16.4	19.1	19.7	39,459
1997	86,106	9.1	7.5	14.3	12.8	16.4	19.0	21.0	40,453
1998	87,212	8.5	7.2	13.5	13.1	16.0	19.5	22.1	41,816
1999	87,671	7.8	7.0	13.9	12.6	16.0	19.1	23.7	42,504

BLACK

1970	6,180	23.4	12.2	20.2	15.8	15.0	9.9	3.6	22,336
1980	8,847	24.0	13.0	18.9	13.8	14.3	11.0	5.0	21,790
1985	9,797	24.5	11.1	18.7	13.3	14.3	11.5	8.6	22,945
1990	10,671	24.8	10.8	16.2	13.5	14.8	12.3	7.6	23,805
1995	11,577	22.0	11.0	17.6	14.2	14.5	12.6	8.0	24,480
1996	12,109	21.8	11.4	17.0	13.9	14.5	13.2	8.2	24,934
1997	12,474	20.7	10.4	17.9	13.9	15.0	13.6	8.5	26,002
1998	12,579	21.1	10.3	17.3	13.6	14.3	13.4	10.0	25,911
1999	12,849	18.5	10.1	16.4	13.7	14.7	14.0	12.6	27,910

HISPANIC[2]

1970	(NA)	(NA)	(NA)	(NA)	(NA)	(NA)	(NA)	(NA)	(NA)
1980	3,906	15.2	10.4	20.2	16.1	16.5	14.9	6.8	27,634
1985	5,213	16.4	11.4	18.9	15.3	16.7	13.2	8.1	27,041
1990	6,220	15.4	10.8	18.4	15.7	17.3	13.6	8.8	28,463
1995	7,939	17.9	11.5	20.4	15.2	14.5	12.6	7.8	24,990
1996	8,225	16.1	11.4	19.9	15.4	15.4	12.7	8.9	26,445
1997	8,590	16.1	10.5	19.5	15.0	16.5	12.5	10.0	27,640
1998	9,060	14.7	10.7	17.8	16.2	15.6	14.3	10.7	28,956
1999	9,319	11.9	9.7	18.9	15.8	16.7	15.2	11.9	30,735

NA: Not available
[1] Includes other races not shown separately.
[2] Persons of Hispanic origin may be of any race.
Source: U.S. Census Bureau, Statistical Abstract of the United States: 2001

These data clearly reveal that the economy of the United States has expanded during the past three or four decades. The question we wish to ask and answer is whether all population groups, and particularly people of color, have participated in an equitable way in this expansion.

Richard Coleman and Lee Rainwater found, in their study *Social Standing in America: New Dimensions of Class,* that people are assigned to various places in the socioeconomic hierarchy by combining such factors as income, occupation, and education (Coleman and Rainwater 1978: 23). Using these three variables, we examine the extent to which parity has been achieved in socioeconomic status between the racial populations of this nation. Since this book is primarily concerned with providing a new perspective on black families, the comparative analysis, in general, is limited to black populations and white populations.

Educational opportunities have improved substantially for all population groups during the last trimester of the twentieth century. We attribute much of this to requirements of the U.S. Supreme Court's 1954 decision in *Brown v. Board of Education* that prohibited racial segregation in public schools operated by public authorities, to affirmative action efforts initiated in educational institutions, and to the Civil Rights Movement.

In the year 2000, 59 percent of all persons twenty-five years old and over had passed middle-range milestones in the educational system: 33.1 percent had earned a high school diploma only; 17.6 percent had attended college but did not obtain a degree; and 7.8 percent had two-year community college degrees only. When this proportion is linked with the proportion of adults who also received college and graduate degrees, we are shown that 84 percent of all employed people twenty-five years of age and over in the United States now have a high school diploma as seen in table 11.2.

Table 11.2 also reveals that 79 percent of black people in the labor force twenty-five years old and over had graduated from high school and 62 percent, a proportion that is similar to the 59 percent for whites, terminated their formal education in the middle range that includes high school graduation only, college attendance without receiving a degree, and a two-year associate arts degree.

The difference between blacks and whites in educational attainment is greatest at both ends of the formal schooling hierarchy. For every 100 black adults, twenty-five years old and over who had less than a high school education, only 70 white adults were similarly situated; and for every 100 black adults who had a bachelor's degree or an advanced degree, 152 to 173 whites had achieved similar levels of formal education. These findings reflect relatively large discrepancies between the two racial populations at the highest and lowest levels.

Data presented in table 11.3a indicate that educational parity, more or less, has been achieved for blacks and whites in the middle range of the formal

Table 11.2. Educational Attainment by Selected Characteristics: 2000. [For persons twenty-five years old and over (175,230 represents 175,230,000). As of March. Based on the Current Population Survey; see Section 1, Population, and Appendix III.]

Characteristic	Population (1,000s)	Not a High School Graduate	High School Graduate	Some College, But No Degree	Associate's Degree	Bachelor's Degree	Advanced Degree
				Percent of Population—Highest Level			
Total Persons	175,230	15.8	33.1	17.6	7.8	17.0	8.6
Age:							
25 to 34 Years Old	37,786	11.8	30.6	19.5	8.8	22.7	6.6
35 to 44 Years Old	44,805	11.4	33.7	18.4	9.5	18.4	8.6
45 to 54 Years Old	36,630	11.1	31.0	18.7	9.0	18.7	11.5
55 to 64 Years Old	23,387	18.3	35.7	16.3	6.2	13.1	10.4
65 to 74 Years Old	17,796	26.4	37.4	14.2	4.5	10.4	7.1
75 Years Old or Over	14,825	35.4	34.1	13.2	3.9	8.7	4.7
Sex:							
Male	83,611	15.8	31.9	17.4	7.1	17.8	10.0
Female	91,620	16.0	34.3	17.7	8.4	16.3	7.3
Race:							
White	147,067	15.1	33.4	17.4	8.0	17.3	8.8
Black	20,036	21.5	35.2	20.0	6.8	11.4	5.1
Other	8,127	16.6	23.8	14.0	7.3	25.2	13.2
Hispanic Origin							
Hispanic	17,150	43.0	27.9	13.5	5.0	7.3	3.3
Non-Hispanic	158,080	13.0	33.7	18.0	8.1	18.1	9.1

Continued

Table 11.2. (Continued)

		Percent of Population—Highest Level					
Characteristic	Population (1,000s)	Not a High School Graduate	High School Graduate	Some College, But No Degree	Associate's Degree	Bachelor's Degree	Advanced Degree
Region:							
Northeast	34,145	15.0	35.3	13.5	7.7	18.0	10.5
Midwest	40,079	13.1	35.5	18.2	8.3	16.8	8.0
South	62,292	18.3	34.0	17.1	7.0	15.7	7.8
West	38,713	15.7	27.4	21.1	8.6	18.6	8.6
Marital status:							
Never Married	26,045	14.9	29.9	17.8	7.5	21.5	8.4
Married Spouse Present	109,296	13.4	33.0	17.4	8.2	18.3	9.8
Married Spouse Absent[2]	2,560	28.0	32.8	14.6	5.5	11.6	7.3
Separated	4,141	24.6	38.0	17.8	6.3	10.1	3.2
Widowed	13,641	35.8	36.1	13.1	4.9	6.8	3.2
Divorced	19,549	13.8	35.4	21.6	8.8	13.3	7.0
Civilian Labor Force Status:							
Employed	114,600	9.7	31.8	18.8	9.0	20.4	10.4
Unemployed	3,908	23.5	36.0	18.7	7.0	10.2	4.7
Not in the Labor Force	56,095	28.3	35.9	14.8	5.4	10.7	5.0

[1] Includes vocational degrees. [2] Excludes those separated.
Source: U.S. Census Bureau, Current Population Reports, P20-536; and unpublished data.

Table 11.3a. Educational Attainment by Race and Gender: United States, 2000 (for persons twenty-five years old and over)

Race and Gender	Less than High School		High School Diploma		Some College, No Degree		College Graduate		Total Employed (1,000)	
	Number	%	Number	%	Number	%	Number	%	Number	%
White Male	5,540		15,536		13,192		16,222		50,444	
White Female	3,169		13,264		12,584		13,067		42,084	
White Total	8,619	9	28,800	31	25,776	28	29,289	32	92,484	100
Black Male	701		2,239		1,792		1,197		5,929	
Black Female	688		2,282		2,273		1,488		6,731	
Black Total	1,389	11	4,521	36	4,065	32	2,685	21	12,660	100
Ratio of %: White/Black		.82		.86		.88		1.52		

education hierarchy. These ratios indicate that for every 100 black persons who graduated from high school only, or who attended college but did not finish a four-year course of study, 86 to 88 white persons had a similar educational experience.

The largest discrepancy in educational accomplishment by race is found among college graduates. For every 100 blacks who completed college only, 152 whites achieved this level of education. Although the college graduation rate gap between the two racial populations is relatively large compared with the narrow gap found for all other levels of educational achievement, we call attention to the fact that the college-educated population in the United States represents only one-quarter of the employed adult population twenty-five years of age and older. All of this is to say that during the past three or four decades, there has been a substantial reduction between the races in the educational attainment gap for 75 percent of the adult population. This is a remarkable achievement.

This finding raises the question as to whether education does as much for black people in terms of employment opportunities as it does for white people. Table 11.3b reveals that a majority of black people in the labor force (51 percent) as well as a majority of white people (63 percent) are now employed in "white collar" jobs. Blacks and whites have almost obtained parity in second tier "white collar" jobs such as technical, sales, and administrative support work. For every 100 blacks in these kinds of jobs, 103 whites are similarly employed. These facts mean that "blue collar" employees, including skilled workers, semiskilled workers, service workers, operatives, fabricators, and labors are now outnumbered by "white collar" workers in the labor force in the Unites States for both racial groups, as revealed in statistical data released for the year 2000, and as seen in table 11.3b.

With the exception of farming (which represents only 2 to 3 percent of the labor force), workers in four of the five remaining major job categories are widely distributed in proportions that reach two digits for both racial groups. Skilled work is an exception to this generalization; only 8 percent of the black population is employed in such jobs. The data in table 11.3b indicate that whites tend to dominate managerial and professional specialty jobs, and skilled worker positions, too. For every 100 black persons employed in the "white collar" top job category of professionals and managers, there are 150 whites so employed. And for every 100 blacks employed in top "blue collar" jobs as skilled workers, there are 150 whites so employed. These two job categories include 48 percent of all whites in the labor force. The proportion of blacks in service work is twice the proportion of whites so employed. Also, for every 100 blacks employed as semiskilled workers and laborers, only 63 white persons also find work in this employment category. The difference may not be sufficiently large to declare that a split labor market by races for all jobs continues to exist in this nation. However, one may truthfully say that

Table 11.3b. Occupations of the Employed by Race and Gender: United States, 2000 (for civilian population twenty-five to sixty-four years old)

Race and Gender	Managerial/ Professional Speciality		Technical/Sales Administrative Support		Service Occupations		Skilled Precision Production/Craft and Repair		Semiskilled Operators/ Fabricators/ Laborers		Farming/ Forestry/ Fishing		Total Employed (1,000)	
	Number	%	Number	%	Number	%	Number	%	Number	%	Number	%	Number	%
White Male	16,390		9,572		3,660		10,410		8,607		1,761		50,400	
White Female	15,682		16,327		5,902		943		2,714		517		42,085	
White Total	32,072	36	25,899	28	9,562	10	11,353	12	11,321	12	2,278	2	92,485	100
Black Male	1,213		1,031		934		915		1,712		125		5,930	
Black Female	1,864		2,386		1,666		150		652		13		6,731	
Black Total	3,077	24	3,417	27	2,600	21	1,065	8	2,364	19	138	1	12,661	100
Ratio of %: White/Black		1.50		1.03		.48		1.50		.63		2.00		

racial selectivity is probably the reason for disparity noted in the job categories discussed above. The highest and lowest occupations in the status hierarchy seem to be dominated by specific racial groups.

A promising sign of progress in the equitable distribution of some jobs in the United States is the racial parity revealed in the second tier category for "white collar" jobs. For every 100 blacks employed in technical, sales, and administrative support positions, 103 whites also are employed in this kind of work. Among service workers, however, the proportion of workers in this employment category is two and one-third times greater (a ratio of 2.3) than the proportion of white service workers.

The educational system and the economic system have responded in somewhat different ways to the equity movement. Schooling in the middle range categories of education—high school graduation only, college study without receiving a degree, and community college completion—is more equitably available than the highly coveted college degree, in which the proportion of whites who are formally recognized for this level of attainment is one-half times greater than the proportion of blacks who accomplish this goal. While the economic system seemed to be less equitable in the distribution of all jobs compared with the more limited amount of inequity in education, as seen in tables 11.3a and 11.3b, the greatest amount of employment inequity in the economic system occurred in the middle-range service and skilled jobs. The "white collar" jobs category (technical, sales, and administration), which seemed to be more equitably distributed among the races, accommodated 28 percent of all workers. And a "blue collar" job category (service work), which seems to be least equitable in the distribution of work by race, accommodated 12 percent of all workers.

At the top end of the educational and the occupational hierarchies, whites were favored in both distributions as seen in tables 11.3a and 11.3b; there were 152 whites for every 100 blacks who complete college only and 150 whites for every 100 blacks employed as managers or professionals.

Analysis of table 4 in connection with tables 11.3a and 11.3b, also, reveal facts that suggest an interaction between educational attainment and employment opportunities. Sixty percent of all college-educated black men and 71 percent of all college-educated black women who earned degrees were employed in professional and managerial jobs at the top of the occupational hierarchy. These proportions are similar to those for whites in which 68 percent of white male college graduates and 72 percent of white female graduates are managers and professionals. Of course, it is possible to be employed as a manager or professional worker without obtaining a college degree. However, this employment opportunity came to only 10 percent of black men and women in the labor force who had not finished college and to only 16 percent of white men and women in the labor force who had not completed a four-year higher-education course of study, as seen in table 11.4.

Table 11.3c. Money Income of Households—Percent Distribution by Income Levels by Race and Gender: United States, 1999 [1999 constant dollars are used in computing income.]

Race and Gender	Under $10,000 Number	%	$10,000–14,999 Number	%	$15,000–24,999 Number	%	$25,000–34,999 Number	%	$35,000–49,999 Number	%	$50,000–74,999 Number	%	$75,000 and Over Number	%	Total (1,000) Number	%
White Male																
White Female																
White Total	6,856	8	6,100	7	12,154	14	11,071	13	13,999	16	16,731	19	20,760	23	87,671	100
Black Male																
Black Female																
Black Total	2,368	18	1,299	10	2,109	16	1,755	14	1,826	15	1,804	14	1,629	13	12,850	100
Ratio of %: White/Black		.44		.70		.88		.93		1.07		1.36		1.77		

Table 11.4. Occupations of the Employed by Selected Characteristics: 2000 [In thousands (59,215 represents 59,215,000). Annual averages of monthly figures. For civilian noninstitutional population twenty-five to sixty-four years old. Based on Current Population Survey; see Section 1, Population, and Appendix III.]

Sex, Race, and Educational Attainment	Total Employed	Managerial/ Professional	Tech./Sales/ Administrative	Service[1]	Precision Production[2]	Operators Fabricators[3]	Farming Forestry Fishing
Male, total[4]	**59,215**	**18,709**	**11,180**	**4,908**	**11,731**	**10,753**	**1,934**
Less than a High School Diploma	6,444	303	447	834	1,904	2,342	615
High School Graduates, No College	18,416	2,100	2,974	1,849	5,386	5,390	718
Less than a Bachelor's Degree	15,606	3,744	3,844	1,603	3,629	2,404	383
College Graduates	18,748	12,562	3,916	622	813	616	218
White	50,400	16,390	9,572	3,660	10,410	8,607	1,761
Less than a High School Diploma	5,450	261	387	596	1,692	1,972	543
High School Graduates, No College	15,536	1,869	2,539	1,316	4,831	4,331	649
Less than a Bachelor's Degree	13,192	3,314	3,258	1,238	3,185	1,838	360
College Graduates	16,222	10,946	3,388	510	702	466	209
Black	5,929	1,213	1,031	934	915	1,712	125
Less than a High School Diploma	701	25	44	160	151	269	52
High School Graduates, No College	2,239	163	314	421	406	881	54
Less than a Bachelor's Degree	1,792	306	422	286	296	468	14
College Graduates	1,197	719	251	67	60	94	5

Female, Total⁴	**51,328**	**18,495**	**19,518**	**7,978**	**1,184**	**3,611**	**542**
Less than a High School Diploma	4,100	255	832	1,707	202	985	120
High School Graduates, No College	16,134	2,330	7,581	3,634	553	1,833	202
Less Than a Bachelor's Degree	15,443	4,569	7,724	2,067	303	635	145
College Graduates	15,651	11,341	3,381	570	127	157	76
White	42,084	15,682	16,327	5,902	943	2,714	517
Less than a High School Diploma	3,169	214	685	1,237	160	760	112
High School Graduates, No College	13,264	2,026	6,548	2,665	455	1,380	191
Less Than a Bachelor's Degree	12,584	3,880	6,320	1,553	231	459	141
College Graduates	13,067	9,562	2,773	447	96	115	73
Black	6,732	1,864	2,386	1,666	150	652	13
Less than a High School Diploma	688	32	102	388	21	140	4
High School Graduates, No College	2,282	235	821	796	69	354	8
Less Than a Bachelor's Degree	2,273	532	1,137	418	46	139	1
College Graduates	1,488	1,064	326	64	13	20	1

¹Includes private household workers. ²Includes craft and repair. ³Includes laborers. ⁴Includes other races, not shown separately. *Source:* U.S. Bureau of Labor Statistics, unpublished data. U.S. Census Bureau, Statistical Abstract of the United States: 2001

If college education is more or less essential in obtaining appointments to professional and managerial jobs, opportunities must open up for more people of color to complete studies for higher-education degrees. We emphasize this fact because a college education seems to be an educational opportunity least available on an equitable basis to black people. As a consequence, professional and managerial jobs are less available to blacks. The proportion of blacks in the labor force who graduated from college now hovers around 16 percent.

Earlier, we mentioned that the relative gains of blacks in income for individuals had improved in a modest way but still is disappointing in terms of equity requirements. Equity in income received is largely experienced by working-class people in black and in white populations. The data in table 11.3c identify the $25,000 to $50,000 range as the income category most fairly available to white people and black people. For every 100 black people who earn between $25,000 and $34,999 a year, there are 93 white people who receive a similar income. And for every 100 black people whose annual compensation for work is from $35,000 to $49,999, 107 white households have a similar experience. In these two income categories, 29 percent of black households and 29 percent of white households are found. Elsewhere in the income hierarchy, equity tends to disappear, with 28 percent of the black population existing on an income of less than $15,000 a year, compared with only 15 percent of the white population that experiences this level of poverty.

It is interesting to note that 27 percent of the black population is now in the two highest income brackets, with 14 percent receiving $50,000 to $74,999 per year and 13 percent receiving $75,000 or more annually. This proportion exceeds one-fourth and is climbing toward the one-third mark. The same proportion of blacks, 28 percent, is found in the lowest two income categories.

The equity analysis of income for households by race dampens any inclinations to celebrate. Table 11.3c reveals that 42 percent of the white people in this nation have annual incomes that exceed $50,000 a year, while 44 percent of black people exist on less than $25,000 a year. There is no justice in this income distribution pattern. This declaration is confirmed by examining the highest and lowest income categories by race. The proportion of black households that exist on less than $10,000 a year (18 percent) is twice as great as the 8 percent of white people who must exist on this paltry sum of money; and the 23 percent of white people who receive $75,000 and more a year is three-quarters greater than the proportion of black with income of a comparable amount.

By race, income in the highest category is distributed in a way that is more inequitable than are the distributions of educational and occupational opportunities in their highest levels. And by race, income in the lowest category is distributed in a way that is more inequitable than are distributions of educational and occupational opportunities in their lowest levels. The distribution of income in this nation cries out for equitable reform.

Examples of inequity are clearly revealed in the data presented in table 11.5 that report 1999 median income by race, while holding educational attainment constant. As may be seen in this table, a gap in median income by race is shown for each educational category. Black individuals with less than a high school education received a median annual income that was $3,054 less than the median annual income received by whites with the same limited amount of education. The median income of black individuals with a high school education only was $4,279 less than that of whites with the same level of education. A difference of $3,546 was seen in the median income of black people and white people who attended college but did not obtain a degree. And the same may be said of blacks and whites who obtained community college degrees for two years of college studies; blacks with this credential receive an annual median income that was $3,914 less than that received by whites with the same educational credential. Black college graduates were not exempt from this discrepancy; they receive a median annual income that was $9,472 less than the median income earned by white college graduates. To summarize, the median income for black people in 1999 was less than that for white people in the United States with a comparable level of education. The median for blacks varied from 80 percent of that for whites among college graduates to 87 or 88 percent, respectively, of that for whites with some college education but no degree or an associate's arts degree from a community college. Again, the largest discrepancy in income between these racial groups was found at the high end of the educational hierarchy among college graduates with bachelor's degrees.

We conclude, based on this analysis, that there is more equity in employment opportunities today than was present a generation ago, that it is inappropriate to classify the labor market as split with certain jobs fully reserved for blacks and others completely reserved for whites, but that a serious amount of selectivity remains that results in greater opportunities available for whites in skilled jobs and greater opportunities available for blacks in service work. This selectivity is most frequently found among workers with a high school diploma only.

Our most important finding is that education serves the employment interests of blacks best among those who have received a college degree. The proportion of college-educated blacks employed as managers, professionals, technician, sales, and administrative workers is similar to the proportion of college-educated whites employed in these jobs. The equity that blacks have experienced is limited more or less to these high-status jobs that require a college education. However, the income they receive from these jobs is not comparable to that received by whites for the same kind of work. Thus, the

Table 11.5. Earnings by Highest Degree Earned: 1999 [For persons eighteen years old and over with earnings. Persons as of March, the following year. Based on Current Population Survey; see Section 1, Population, and Appendix.]

Characteristic	Total Persons	Level of Highest Degree							
		Not a High School Graduate	High School Graduate Only	Some College, No Degree	Associate's	Bachelor's	Master's	Professional	Doctorate
MEAN EARNINGS (dollars)									
All Persons[1]	**32,356**	**16,121**	**24,572**	**26,958**	**32,152**	**45,678**	**55,641**	**100,987**	**86,833**
Age									
25 to 34 Years Old	29,901	16,916	24,040	26,914	28,088	39,768	46,768	58,043	60,852
35 to 44 Years Old	36,900	18,984	27,444	34,219	35,370	50,153	56,816	100,240	94,936
45 to 54 Years Old	41,465	19,707	28,883	36,935	37,508	54,922	62,158	116,327	87,659
55 to 64 Years Old	38,577	22,212	27,558	34,240	35,703	50,141	57,580	132,326	97,214
65 Years Old or Over	24,263	12,121	18,704	19,052	17,609	30,624	35,639	104,055	78,333

Sex									
Male	40,257	18,855	30,414	33,614	40,047	57,706	68,367	120,352	97,357
Female	23,551	12,145	18,092	20,241	25,079	32,546	42,378	59,792	61,136
White	33,326	16,623	25,270	27,674	32,686	46,894	55,622	103,450	87,746
Male	41,598	19,320	31,279	34,825	41,010	59,606	68,831	123,086	97,076
Female	23,756	12,405	18,381	20,188	24,928	32,507	41,845	57,314	64,080
Black	24,979	13,569	20,991	24,101	28,772	37,422	48,777	75,509	(B)
Male	28,821	16,391	25,849	27,538	31,885	42,530	54,642	(B)	(B)
Female	21,694	10,734	16,506	21,355	26,787	33,184	44,761	(B)	(B)
Hispanic[2]	22,096	16,106	20,704	23,115	29,329	36,212	50,576	64,029	(B)
Male	24,970	18,020	23,736	27,288	36,740	42,733	60,013	(B)	(B)
Female	18,187	12,684	16,653	18,782	22,695	29,249	41,118	(B)	(B)

Base figure too small to meet statistical standards for reliability of a derived figure. [1]Includes other races, not shown separately. [2]Persons of Hispanic origin may be of any race.

Source: U.S. Census Bureau, Current Population Reports, P20-536.

parity that we found in employment opportunities is restricted to about one-sixth (16 percent) of the black adult population that has graduated from college. Of the remaining 84 to 85 percent of blacks twenty-five years old and over, there is modest selectivity in employment opportunities that favor whites in skilled jobs and that favor blacks in service work. Semiskilled and laboring jobs seem to be more or less available to all racial groups in an equitable way.

While higher education has helped blacks close the gap more and more in job opportunities available to them compared with whites, thus far the gap in income received by blacks that lags up to 20 percentage points behind that received by whites continues today. While the income differential is not as great today as it was in years gone by, it continues and is a challenge to this nation to eliminate the residual inequities in education, employment, and income.

V

CONCLUSIONS

12

Interdependent Social Classes and Family Adaptations

Our conclusions deal with important issues analyzed in this book: (1) the stratification of black families and the methods and techniques used by varying strata to attain success; (2) the stratification of black families and the orientation of specific families and groups of families in varying strata toward humanistic values such as service, sacrifice, and suffering; and (3) the new egalitarian family form that seems to be emerging among black families and its implications for role behavior of spouses and power relations between family members. Finally, we shall offer our observations based on data presented regarding whether race continues to be a significant variable affecting the interaction and adaptation of black families to the macrosocial organization of society in the United States.

STRATIFICATION AND SUCCESS

Our data show that blacks in all socioeconomic status levels are interested in being successful. However, each stratum seeks to attain success in different ways and for different reasons.

Affluent or middle-class black families are strong believers in what Max Weber calls "the Protestant ethic and spirit of capitalism" (Weber 1930). Middle-class blacks believe that success or the accumulation of material wealth is a function of honesty, punctuality, hard work, diligence, and frugality (Weber 1930: 52). Indeed, middle-class blacks believe they have to be twice as good as others in order to succeed. Thus, they are very much committed to their work.

These values and virtues mentioned above are found among middle-class white people and other races, too. However, among members of the white middle class, these virtues and values are beneficial "only insofar . . . as they are actually useful to the individual" (Weber 1930: 52). Also, in white middle-class families, appearance of the presence of these values rather than the reality of them is sufficient, if they accomplish the desired end (Weber 1930: 52).

Although black middle-class people believe that they must run twice as fast as others to catch up, they are reluctant to try shortcuts. These values and virtues for them are real and contribute to their commitment to work. They believe in traditional definitions of success and proven methods for its attainment.

A very important difference between racial groups in the United States has to do with the reasons for striving for success. As mentioned earlier, among some racial groups these virtues and values mentioned are adopted because they are useful to individuals striving for success. However, among black middle-class families, these values and virtues are pursued because they are beneficial to the individual as well as the racial group with which one identifies. For example, the mother in the Allen family case study believed that her employment in a suburban school district near Philadelphia was "making a difference." She believed that the little white children she taught would grow up knowing that "people are people" and that skin color doesn't matter. Beverly Allen's goal was not limited to teaching her students subject matter. Her goal was to change the thinking of the children and, hopefully, the thinking of their parents. Thus, Mrs. Allen wants to make a difference through her work to enlighten white people about the potentialities of people in her racial group.

The attitude of Mrs. Allen about the value of her work as a teacher in the suburbs as a way of uplifting her race is similar to the attitude expressed by Halle Berry who won the coveted Oscar award for best female actress during the 74th Academy Awards ceremony on March 24, 2002, in Los Angeles. Berry was the first black female to ever win an honor in the best actress category. Her acceptance speech was described by *Jet* magazine as "emotional" and "heartwarming" (*Jet*, 8 April 2002: 16). This, in part, is what she said: "Oh, my God . . . this moment is so much bigger than me. This moment is for . . . the women who stand beside me . . . and it's for every nameless, faceless woman of color that now has a chance because this door tonight has been opened. . . . I'm so honored and I thank the Academy for choosing me to be the vessel for which [God's] blessing may flow. . . . Thank you, thank you, thank you!"

Both the speech of Halle Berry and the testimony of Beverly Allen indicate that affluent and/or middle-class blacks interpret their success as having a meaning that goes beyond the individual, a meaning that benefits a race of people. Halle Berry characterized herself as a vessel through which the blessings of God flowed for the purpose of opening the door of recognition for other women of color.

During the same Academy Awards ceremony, "actor Sidney Poitier received an honorary Oscar for his trailblazing movie career. He made history as the first black man to win an Oscar for his staring role in the 1963 classic [motion picture], *Lilies of the Field*" (*Jet*, 8 April 2002: 53). And this, in part, is what Denzel Washington, winner of the best actor Oscar that was awarded the same evening, had to say: "God is good, God is great. God is great. From the bottom of my heart, I thank you all. Forty years I've been chasing Sidney [Poitier]. . . . I'll always be chasing you, Sidney. I'll always be following in your footsteps. There's nothing [else] I would rather do, sir. Nothing I would rather do. God bless you. God bless you" (*Jet*, 8 April 2002:51).

Washington's statement clearly revealed that what Poitier (the first black man to receive an Oscar for best actor) did forty years ago had inspired and motivated him continuously. Washington was the second black man to be so honored. These words and the analysis of the case studies in this book indicate that the work activity of middle-class and/or affluent black family members has a function in society that transcends individual success. As middle-class blacks see it, the good that they accomplish personally should be generalized as a racial achievement.

Moreover, middle-class blacks are not reluctant to describe their success as a manifestation of divine purpose. References to God in the acceptance speeches of both honorees for best actor and actress indicate a deep and abiding religious faith that is found among many middle-class black people. Weber has said that "a calling," that which one is commissioned to do, is "central dogma of all Protestant denominations" (Weber 1930: 80). One could say "the calling [is] . . . the task set by God" (Weber 1930: 85). So Denzel Washington began his Oscar acceptance speech by declaring, "God is good, God is great." Likewise, Halle Berry began her Oscar acceptance speech with the exclamation, "Oh, my God!" These comments indicate that effective fulfillment of a calling has a purpose greater than each individual.

The middle-class black families in the case studies in this book were churchgoing people; some members of the Hart family attended church services once a week, and others attended twice a month. All Allen family members attended church services weekly. A 1985 study of middle-class black families revealed that most of these families were affiliated with churches and attended them weekly or occasionally, with a majority falling into the weekly category (Willie 1985: 296). Among most middle-class black families, it is fair to characterize religion as something good for them that, from their perspectives, has contributed to their success.

Working-class black families, also, are interested in success. However, they doubt that they can find success through their own jobs. Income from laboring, semiskilled, and service work is so low that both husband and wife are required to work with one spouse sometimes holding more than one job to provide for the children. The innovative strategies used by working-class blacks to keep their families afloat are remarkable.

A good education for their children is the aspiration of most working-class black families. They expect the children to fulfill the family's hope for upward mobility, and they invest in their children to the fullest of their capacity. For example, the father in the Todd family case study "tries to give his children everything he missed in his young life." And the mother visits school regularly to check on the progress of her children and how they are treated.

Working-class black families have few contacts with any community institutions except church and school. For some working-class black families, religion helps them adapt to hard times. They conceptualize misfortunes as tests by God who eventually will see them through any storm, according to the Todd family.

Church, also, is important in the way of life of the Banks family. The parents believe that their handicapped daughter is "one of God's handiworks." They declare that their strong faith in God "is sustaining."

Coping with long hours of work, disability, and other misfortunes, these working-class black families are hard-pressed to participate in religious activities as often as they may wish. The 1985 study of black families mentioned above indicates that about one-third of black working-class families attend church weekly, about one-third occasionally, and that about one-third never attend church.

Finally, our data show that low-income black families, also, are interested in success. But success for them is elusive, is more or less limited to rescuing family and friends who are down on their luck and would otherwise perish if not given a helping hand.

Low-income black family members continue to be the last hired and the first fired. Their frequent loss of jobs leaves them without healthcare insurance and other protections. Public welfare assistance is hard to get, as is reliable day care for children of mothers who want to work. These are liabilities chronicled in the Roby family case study. While the children are "very important" to Mrs. Roby, about the most she can hope for in educational achievement is high school graduation.

Beyond family members, low-income blacks have few people to turn to for help. One does not have many close friends in neighborhoods characterized by high crime and drug activity. There is belief among some low-income blacks that if they are too trusting they will be used by others.

Church as a community agency is probably more important to low-income black people than religion as dogma. The mother in the Roby family was able to "make ends meet" by visiting community food pantries and clothing thrift shops operated by churches. And the Marsh family was provided housing for the family as well as a job for the husband by the City Mission Society (a religious association) to help the family stabilize after the father was released from a psychiatric hospital. A 1985 study of low-income black families revealed that they usually are all for or all against organized religion; about 50 percent attend church weekly and about 50 percent attend occasionally or never (Willie 1985: 296).

It is their religious orientation, however, that helps poor people reach out and redeem family members or friends who have fallen. This is redemptive work that begins by accepting people who are "down and out" as they are, that forgives those in need of help for their past follies, and that suffers with their misfortune as they struggle "to get back on their feet."

The case studies presented in this book indicate that low-income black families need "safety nets" to protect them from the vicissitudes of life. Secular institutions seem to have given up on the poor. Thus, religious institutions are left to help meet their needs that require more resources than most inner-city churches have.

When a family confronts hardships piled high and deep, it is difficult to plan for the future. And yet, this is precisely what low-income black families do when they rebel and rage against society for ignoring their unique and special needs. Because the poor are invisible to most people in a common community, their rebellious activity seems to be the only way they can get society at large to pay attention to them and help. The poor cannot overcome the effects of poverty alone, without assistance from others. Getting the sympathetic attention of others whose help is necessary and essential, is one indicator of success for black low-income families.

STRATIFICATION AND HUMANISTIC VALUES

Beyond striving for success, we find that social stratification among black people is related to other humanistic values such as service to others, sacrifice for others, and suffering with others. Our comparative research on black families and white families indicates that these humanistic values also are found among white families and tend to vary by social class in a similar way as they vary among blacks.

Data gathered from case studies in this book and from case studies in a 1985 study (Willie 1985) will be analyzed to show how service, sacrifice, and suffering are manifested among black families.

Service, sacrifice, and suffering are human adaptations that are necessary and essential in social organizations. Without participants willing to function in these ways, a society could not long endure. A society devoid of altruistic, generous, magnanimous sharing manifested in specific action strategies of service, sacrifice, and suffering, could not continue to exist. Such a society would consist either of egocentric people seeking only individual enhancement but not group advancement or of ethnocentric people seeking only group advancement but not individual enhancement.

Service to society is an idea that middle-class families have refined and implemented, as seen in the case histories in this study. They give freely of their time and effort to organizations and associations created to uplift and give security to others.

Middle-class families, as institution-building people, create organizations and associations as necessary and essential components of society. They understand how vulnerable is the individual acting alone. They are disinclined to leave personal security to chance. Thus, they dedicate their lives to service of others by supporting institutional systems that in the end benefit not only them but also the society at large. Middle-class families are capable of rendering the services that they give because the resources they command are more than sufficient for survival. They, therefore, are free to devote part of their time to altruistic activities. The father in a black middle-class family that recently moved to the suburbs serves on a chamber of commerce committee that sets up "big brother" partnerships between successful corporations and new minority companies. This person describes his volunteer work as "the single most rewarding thing I have done" since moving into his new community.

That race is on the mind of many middle-class blacks is further indicated by the kinds of community groups with which adults in these families are affiliated: the Black Citizens Association, the local Democratic Committee, the National Alliance for Business, and the National Association for the Advancement of Colored People. Their reason for joining these groups, some middle-class blacks say, is to improve the condition of black people (Willie 1985: 283). Hart family members, discussed in this book, are members of a church and several sports associations for the children. Moreover, one parent is affiliated with a graduate chapter of a fraternity and the State Public Administration Association. Middle-class people who offer these services do so because they are generous, service-oriented people who usually give more than they are required to give.

While middle-class families are freer to render service and teach others through their actions the meaning of altruism, working-class families help us to understand the significance of sacrifice. Working-class parents, particularly those who appear in the case studies of this book, were models of sacrificial giving. They wanted their children to experience life with fewer hardships and greater opportunities. They wanted their offspring to outachieve them, to be upwardly mobile, to get ahead. Through hard work, the parents tried to provide a home that was safe and secure for children coming of age. Their children, they believe, need time to learn so that eventually they can earn enough to be independent. The working-class families also sacrifice their privacy when a small house is shared with relatives who are down on their luck and need temporary shelter.

However, it is through their children that working-class families hope to contribute to society. In supporting and sustaining their households, the parents work as long and as much as they can. Their labor is human capital. It is all that they have to invest in a better way of life for others. They freely sacrifice it for the sake of others, expecting nothing in return except the satisfaction of seeing the younger generation prosper and experience the success that eluded their parents. Such sacrifice is something of value. Working-class families sacrifice for their children so that they may grow up to be "self-sufficient," "independent," "well-behaved," "respectable" survivors who are better off than their parents (Willie 1985: 155).

Working-class people are magnanimous in that they tend to take less than they are entitled. This is the essence of sacrifice that working-class families have taught our society.

While working-class people are magnanimous in their sacrificial offerings, the poor with little to give and much to gain can teach us how to endure and suffer the redemption of the fallen. Unable to transform society through service and with few, if any, resources to sacrifice, the poor reach out to others in need and sustain them by their presence, shouldering their burdens and sharing their grief as if it were their own. They share by caring and showing concern. Experience has demonstrated that sorrow divided among many is easier to bear. Thus, the poor suffer the redemption of those who have fallen by direct participation in their lives, by sharing their misfortune.

There is an immediacy to the manner in which the poor in this study responded to the problems of others. They know how to be a present help in time of trouble. The redemptive consequences of shared suffering are remarkable—a lesson that should be learned by all. The Marsh family in this book is a classic example of how a wife suffered the redemption of her husband from diseased and delinquent behavior.

Service, sacrifice, and suffering are adaptive strategies perfected by the people of one social class but necessary learning for others. In this respect the affluent, the working-class, and the poor are interdependent. Each group has learned a way of adapting that can be taught to others. These adaptive strategies are not properties of any social class. No group deserves to have the experiences that it has had. However, successes as well as failures in the adaptations of any group are experiential lessons that can be learned by others. Because the members of all social classes must serve, sacrifice, and suffer at some time in life, it is well that they learn how to make these adaptations from the groups in society that already have had such experiences. Thus, society may endure, transcend, and transform itself only if it uses the wisdom of all its people—including the poor who teach others how to suffer, the working class who teach others how to sacrifice, and the affluent who teach others how to serve. Each group has something to teach and learn from all others as revealed in this study of interdependent social classes.

THE GAP IN EDUCATION, OCCUPATION, AND INCOME

For about a quarter of a century, social scientists have debated the proposition that race has declined as a significant variable that affects the life-chances of people of color. Some scholars present evidence that it has not declined as a significant variable in the United States, while others present evidence that it has declined. Our findings in this book reveal two important facts about this matter: (1) *there is no parity* between black populations and white populations in some levels of educational attainment, in some occupational categories, and in some income ranges; and (2) *there is parity* between black populations and white populations in some levels of educational attainment, in some occupational categories, and in some income ranges. We begin by explaining how these contrasting statements apply to education as an institutional system in our society.

There is virtual parity between these two racial groups (blacks and whites) at two levels of educational attainment: adults with a high school diploma only and adults who attended college but did not receive a degree. For every 100 black adults with some college education but no degree, there are 88 white adults who have had the same experience; for every 100 black adults with a high school diploma only, there are 86 white adults with the same level of educational attainment. Less than 15 percentage points separate black populations and white populations at these levels of educational attainment in the United States. Thus, we conclude that there is almost parity here. It is interesting to note that the 8,586,000 adults with educational attainment at these two levels were two-thirds (67.8 percent) of the total employed population during the year 2000.

At the level of lowest educational attainment (adults who did not finish high school), the difference between blacks and whites is still modest. For every 100 blacks with a low level of educational attainment, there are 82 whites with similar experiences. This difference is described as modest because it is less than 20 percentage points.

We conclude that there is a fair amount of equity in the distributions of black and white populations by education in all levels from the lowest up through the level of some college but no degree. The absence of equity is seen largely at one educational level, that of college graduation. There are 152 whites for every 100 blacks who have earned a college degree. This figure represents a large discrepancy of racial opportunity for all to access higher education. This is a wrong on the throne that sways the future, to paraphrase James Russell Lowell, and should be redressed by this nation.

By occupations, parity between black and white population groups is seen for only one category—technical, sales, and administrative support workers. For every 100 black workers who pursue occupations in this category, there are 103 white workers so employed. For all other categories of work, there are gross proportional discrepancies by race.

White workers dominate three employment categories: (1) managerial and professional specialties; (2) skilled work, including crafts, trades, and repair; and (3) farming, forestry, and fishing. In the top "white collar" and in the top "blue collar" job categories (managerial and professional specialties and skilled work), there are 150 whites employed for every 100 blacks pursuing such work. The two occupational categories dominated by blacks are, in general, "blue collar" jobs. For every 100 blacks in service occupations, there are only 48 whites; for every 100 blacks in semiskilled work, including fabricators, operators, and laborers, there are only 63 whites in the same occupations. Thus, we conclude that in the year 2000, one-quarter (27 percent) of black workers had achieved parity with white workers and three-quarters (73 percent) had not.

Again, in the middle range, from $15,000 to $49,999, blacks have more or less experienced equity with whites in annual income: 16 percent of blacks and 14 percent of whites have annual incomes of $15,000 to $24,999; 14 percent of blacks and 13 percent of whites have incomes of $25,000 to $34,999; and 15 percent of blacks and 16 percent of whites have incomes from $35,000 to $49,999. Thus, we conclude that 45 percent of all black households have more or less attained proportional equity with white households in annual income received, while 55 percent have not. The most severe racial discrepancy is at both ends of the income range. At $75,000 and above, there are 177 white households to every 100 black households who receive this amount of money annually. And, at the other end of the range (less than $10,000 annually), there are only 44 whites to every 100 blacks who exist on less than a $1,000 a month.

To summarize, we conclude that two-thirds of blacks (68 percent) have more or less attained equity in educational attainment with whites, that one-quarter of blacks (27 percent) have attained equity in job occupations with whites, and that nearly half of all blacks (45 percent) have more or less attained equity in annual income with whites. In all instances, equity was attained in the middle-range categories for the education, occupation, and income variable. Gross proportional inequities by race that favor whites still continue in the top categories, including college graduation, managerial and professional specialties, and annual income of $75,000 and above.

THE EGALITARIAN FAMILY

Finally, our study reveals that the egalitarian family form, in which neither spouse is always in charge, is a new contribution to this society that has emerged largely from the black experience.

The assertion by Daniel Patrick Moynihan that "ours is a society which presumes male leadership in private and public affairs" (U.S. Department of Labor 1965: 29) disregarded the findings of Russell Middleton and Snell Putney (Middleton and Putney 1960: 605–609) published five years before the Moynihan report. A reanalysis of the Middleton and Putney data in chapter 9 of this book revealed that an equalitarian pattern of decision making appeared to be the norm for most American households and that black middle-class and black working-class families have given leadership in development of this emerging domestic custom. Families in these two status groups seem to be the most flexible in sharing decision-making authority among spouses, with neither wife nor husband always dominating. Of all race-class groups, the most equalitarian in decision making is the middle-class black family. Instead of male dominance in the family being the ideal type, as asserted by Moynihan, supreme dominance by husband or wife would appear to be a cultural lag rapidly giving way to equalitarian cultural patterns.

Adaptations in minority population groups often reflect the best and worst possibilities in a society. The equalitarian, power-sharing family structure that has emerged in black families is a good pattern worthy of replication by all. This structure, which involves the participation of both parents in child-rearing and home-management decisions, is a contribution by black people to the ongoing process of family reform in the United States.

While exalting equalitarian, power-sharing households most frequently found among black families, we are mindful of the fact that intact families with both parents present in households seem to be less frequently found among blacks than among whites. Walter Allen attributes this phenomenon both to economic circumstances and to cultural norms that independently and jointly affect family stability (Allen 1987: 171).

It is a well-known fact that the number of intact families consisting of married couples tends to increase as the level of family income increases. Thus, we are more inclined to attribute the lower rate of intact families among black people compared with white people to the different economic circumstances of these two population groups. Economic resources, as shown in chapter 11, are substantially greater among whites than among blacks.

The *Statistical Abstract of the United States* has a table of data on the marital status of the population by race (U.S. Census Bureau 2000: 51). It shows that the greater difference between the proportion of black and white people over eighteen years of age who are married (41.4 percent for blacks and 62 percent for whites in 1999) is probably more a function of a large minority of blacks (39.2 percent) who never married than a function of divorce or widowhood (11.9 percent and 7.6 percent, respectively) among blacks in 1999. Whites of this same age category who never married were only 21.4 percent of their population eighteen years and older; and the proportions of divorced and widowed among whites were 6 percent and 8 percent, respectively in 1999. Eighteen percentage points separated these two racial populations in proportions never married, but only 1 to 6 percentage points separated them in the proportions divorced or widowed (U.S. Census Bureau 2000: 51). For this reason, we believe that the "never married" variable tends to influence the "married" variable more than it is influenced by the "divorced" and widowed" variables.

Since the proportion of people eighteen years of age and over who are married has decreased in both populations during the past few decades (1980 to 1999) by 5 percentage points for whites and 10 percentage points for blacks (U.S. Census Bureau 2000: 51), and because this decrease is matched by an increase in proportion never married between 1980 and 1999 from 3 percentage points for whites to 9 percentage points for blacks, we conclude that one should be cautious about attributing rate differentials in family structures between blacks and whites to cultural factors unless one controls for socioeconomic experiences that have not reached parity between these racial groups. Caution should be exercised in attributing marriage and divorce rate differences to cultural customs because we know that a positive correlation exists between rates of family affluence and rates of intact families.

In addition to reconfirming what we already know about the association between status-attainment and family stability, we believe, based on data and their analysis in this book, that a new fruitful line of research should explore the relationship between family structure and changing power relationships within families. Our hypothesis is that the decreasing rate of married couples in the Unites States is probably associated with the increasing rate of equality among men and women in family decision making. Because this is a relatively new experience, a little more than one generation old in our society, we have not developed effective methods for negotiating differences between equal marital partners. Without tried and true negotiating strategies, when a couple of adults with shared power reach an impasse, they tend to separate if they have no knowledge or customary ways of repairing a strained intimate relationship. If this hypothesis is confirmed, it could become a finding that helps us understand one reason, among others, that the rate of family breakup is higher among black people. They are pioneers; they are among the early explorers of this relatively new egalitarian family form and, therefore, are experiencing the consequences of participating in an emerging cultural arrangement of powersharing between spouses who are equal before adequate guidelines have developed regarding what to do during a crisis.

In due time, more families in other racial, socioeconomic, and cultural groups will adopt the equalitarian, power-sharing format most frequently seen among blacks and, also, will experience the same debilitating outcomes such as family breakups more frequently experienced by blacks. Eventually, the culture will develop prescriptions and other customary or normative ways of managing disagreements among spouses with equal power; and a new equilibrium in family relations will emerge. We predict this will happen because most studies have found that more people are satisfied in egalitarian families than in any other family form.

References

Addison, Donald. 1983. Black Wives: Perspective About Their Husbands and Themselves. In *Black Marriage and Family Therapy*, ed. Constance E. Obudho, 91–111. Westport, Conn.: Greenwood Press.

Allen, Walter 1983. Differences in Husband-Wife Interpersonal Relationships During the Middle Years of Marriage. In *Black Marriage and Family Therapy*, ed. Constance E. Obudho, 75–89. Westport, Conn.: Greenwood Press.

Allen, Walter R. 1987. Black Family, White Family: A Comparison of Family Organization. In *The Color Line and the Quality of Life in America*, Reynolds Farley and Walter R. Allen, 160–187. New York: Russell Sage Foundation.

Allport, Gordon W. 1955. *Becoming*. New Haven, Conn.: Yale University Press.

Appleton, William. 1981. *Fathers and Daughters*. Garden City, N.Y.: Doubleday.

Auletta, Ken. 1982. *The Underclass*. New York: Random House.

Bacon, Francis. 1973. *The Advancement of Learning*. London: J. M. Dent and Sons.

Barnes, Annie. 1983. Black Husbands and Wives: An Assessment of Marital Roles in a Middle-Class Neighborhood. In *Black Marriage and Family Therapy*, ed. Constance E. Obudho, 55–73. Westport, Conn.: Greenwood Press.

Biller, Henry. 1974. *Parental Deprivation*. Lexington, Mass.: Lexington Books.

———. 1976. The Father-Child Relationship: Some Crucial Issues. In *The Family—Can it be Saved?* ed. Victor C. Vaughan III and T. Berry Brazelton, 69–76. Chicago, Ill.: Year Book Medical Publishers.

Billingsley, Andrew. 1968. *Black Families in White America*. Englewood Cliffs, N.J.: Prentice-Hall.

Black Enterprise Research. 2002. 2002 B.E. Industrial/Service. http://blackenterprise.com/BE100sItem.asp?Id=is200200. Cited 27 October 2002.

Blau, Peter M. 1987. Contrasting Theoretical Perspectives. In *The Micro-Micro Link*, ed. Jeffrey C. Alexander, Richard Giesen, Richard Münch, and Neil J. Smelser, 71–85. Berkeley, Calif.: University of California Press.

Blau, Peter M., and Otis D. Duncan. 1967. *The American Occupational Structure*. New York: The Free Press.

Bogdan, Robert C., and Sari Knopp Biklen. 1982. *Qualitative Research for Education.* Boston: Allyn and Bacon.

Brashers, Freda, and Margaret Roberts. 1996. The Black Church as a Resource for Change. In *The Black Family: Strengths, Self-Help, and Positive Change,* ed. Sadye L. Logan. Boulder, Colo.: Westview Press.

Chute, Carolyn. 1985. *The Beans of Egypt, Maine.* New York: Ticknor.

Coleman, Richard P., and Lee Rainwater. 1978. *Social Standing in America.* New York: Basic Books.

Coles, Robert. 1965. There's Sinew in the Negro Family. Paper presented at White House Conference on Civil Rights. Reprinted in *The Washington Post,* 10 October 1965.

Conway, Jill K. 1992. *Written by Herself.* New York: Vintage.

Cook, Samuel Dubois. 1971. Introduction, Reflections on a Rebel's Journey. In *Born to Rebel,* B. E. Mays. New York: Charles Scribner Sons.

Cottle, Thomas J. 1975. *A Family Album.* New York: Harper and Row.

Cox, Harvey. 1969. Feasibility and Fantasy: Sources of Social Transcendence. In *Transcendence,* ed. H. W. Richardson and D. L. Cutler. Boston: Beacon Press.

Denby, Ramona W. 1996. Resilience and the African American Family: A Model of Family Preservation. In *The Black Family: Strengths, Self-Help, and Positive Change,* ed. Sadye L. Logan. Boulder, Colo.: Westview Press.

Douglass, Frederick. 1962. *Life and Times of Frederick Douglass.* 1892. New York: Macmillan.

DuBos, René. 1968. *So Human an Animal.* New York: Charles Scribner Sons.

Duncan, Beverly, and O. D. Duncan. 1970. Family Stability and Occupational Success. In *The Family Life of Black People,* ed. C. V. Willie, 156–171. Columbus, Ohio: Merrill.

Duncan, Otis Dudley. 1961. A Sociological Index for All Occupations and Properties and Characteristics of the Socioeconomic Index. In *Occupations and Social Status,* ed. Albert Reiss. New York: Free Press.

Edwards, G. Franklin, ed. 1968. *Franklin Frazier on Race Relations.* Chicago: University of Chicago Press.

Farkas, George. 1996. *Human Capital or Cultural Capital?* New York: Aldine de Gruyter.

Farkas, George, Christy Llevas, and Steve Maczuga. 2002. Does Oppositional Culture Exist in Minority and Poverty Peer Groups? *American Sociological Review* 67:148–155.

Farley, Reynolds. 1995. Introduction. In *State of the Union,* vol. 2: Social Trends, ed. Reynolds Farley, ix–xvii. New York: Russell Sage Foundation.

Farley, Reynolds, and Walter Allen. 1987. *The Color Line and the Quality of Life in America.* New York: Russell Sage Foundation.

Fletcher, Joseph. 1967. *Moral Responsibility.* Philadelphia: The Westminster Press.

Fordham, Signithia, and John Ogbu. 1986. Black Students' School Success: Coping with the Burden of 'Acting White.' *Urban Review* 18:176–206.

Foreman, Judy. 1993. The Mother-Daughter Bond. *Boston Sunday Globe,* 9 May 1993, pp. 1, 12.

Frazier, E. Franklin. 1939. *The Negro Family in the United States.* Chicago: University of Chicago Press.

————. 1957. *Black Bourgeoisie*. New York: Free Press.

Friday, N. 1977. *My Mother/Myself*. New York: Dell.

Geisen, Ludwig. 1973. 1973. *555 Families*. New Brunswick, N.J.: Transaction Books.

Glasgow, Douglas G. 1980. *The Black Underclass*. San Francisco: Jossey-Bass.

Haley, Alex. 1976. *Roots, The Saga of an American Family*. Garden City, N.Y.: Doubleday.

Harris, Louis. 1987. *Inside America*. New York: Vintage Books.

Heilbrun, Alfred B., Jr. 1972. An Empirical Test of the Modeling Theory of Sex-Role Learning. In *Readings on the Family System*, ed. Ira L. Reiss, 49–59. New York: Holt, Rinehart and Winston.

Hennig, Margaret, and A. Jardin. 1976. *The Managerial Woman*. New York: Pocket Books.

Hill, Robert. 1977. *The Strength of Black Families*. New York: Emerson Hall.

————. 1999. *The Strengths of African American Families: Twenty-Five Years Later*. Lanham, Md.: University Press of America.

Hollingshead, A. B. 1949. *Elmtown's Youth*. New York: John Wiley and Sons.

Huxley, Julian. 1929. *Essays of a Biologist*. New York: Alfred A. Knopf.

Jackson, Jacquelyne J. 1973. Black Women in a Racist Society. In *Racism and Mental Health*, ed. C. V. Willie, B. M. Kramer, and B. S. Brown, 185–268. Pittsburgh: University of Pittsburgh Press.

Jeffers, Camille. 1970. Mother and Children in Public Housing. In *The Family Life of Black People*, ed. Charles V. Willie. Columbus, Ohio: Charles E. Merrill.

Jet. 2002. Halle Berry Gives Thanks for Her Historic Oscar Win. 8 April. 101, no. 16:14–18, 51–61.

Johnson, John H. 1992. *Succeeding Against the Odds: The Autobiography of a Great American Businessman*. New York: Amistad Press.

King, Martin Luther, Jr. 1958. *Stride Toward Freedom*. New York: Harper and Row.

Landry, Bart. 1987. *The Black Middle-Class*. Berkeley, Calif.: University of California Press.

————. 2000. *Black Working Wives*. Berkeley, Calif.: University of California Press.

Leighton, Alexander H. 1946. *The Governing of Men*. Princeton, N.J.: Princeton University Press.

Leik, Robert K. 1972. Instrumentality and Emotionality in Family. In *Readings on the Family System*, ed. Ira L. Reiss, 257–269. New York: Rineholt and Winston.

Lewis, Jerry M., and John G. Looney. 1983. *The Long Struggle: Well-Functioning Working-Class Black Families*. New York: Brunner/Mazel.

Lynd, Robert, and Helen Merrell. 1929. *Middletown*. New York: Harcourt Brace Jovanovich.

MacDonald, Michael P. 1999. *All Souls, A Family Story From Southie*. New York: Ballantine.

Mack, Delores. 1978. The Power Relationship in Black Families and White Families. In *The Black Family*, ed. R. Staples. Belmont, Calif.: Wadsworth.

Mays, Benjamin E. 1963. *Quotable Quotes of Benjamin E. Mays*. New York: Vantage Press.

————. 1971. *Born to Rebel*. New York: Charles Scribner's Sons.

Merton, Robert K. 1949. *Social Theory and Social Structure*. New York: Free Press.

————. 1968. *Social Theory and Social Structure*. New York: Free Press. Revised edition.

Middleton, Russell, and Snell Putney. 1960. Dominance in Decisions in the Family: Race and Class Differences. *American Journal of Sociology* 65, no. 6:605–609.

Milgam, Stanley. 1974. *Obedience to Authority*, New York: Harper and Row.

Morgan, James, and Associates. 1962. *Income and Welfare in the United States*. New York: McGraw-Hill.

Moyers, Bill. 1986. The Vanishing Black Family—A Crisis in Black America. Televised documentary.

Murphy, Michael. 1974. Education for Transcendence. In *Transcendence*, ed. H. W. Richardson and D. L. Cutler. Boston, Mass.: Beacon Press.

O'Connor, Carla. 2000. Dreamkeeping in the Inner City: Diminishing the Divide Between Aspiration and Expectation. In *Coping with Poverty: The Social Contest of Neighborhood, Work, and Family in the African-American Community*, ed. Sheldon Danziger and Ann Chih Lin. Ann Arbor: University of Michigan Press.

Oliver, Melvin, and Thomas Shapiro. 1995. *Black Wealth/White Wealth*. New York: Routledge.

Perlman, Janice. 1976. *The Myth of Marginality*. Berkeley: University of California Press.

Reynolds, Pamela. 1985. Black Men-Black Women: The Expectation Gap. *Boston Globe* 22 September, pp. B23, B25.

Rodman, Hyman. 1971. *Lower-Class Families: The Culture of Poverty in Negro Trinidad*. London: Oxford University Press.

Scanzoni, John H. 1971. *The Black Family in Modern Society*. Boston: Allyn and Bacon.

Schofer, Evan, and Marion Fourcade-Gourinchas. 2001. The Structural Context of Civic Engagement: Voluntary Association Membership in Comparative Perspective. *American Sociological Review* 66, no. 6:806–828.

Schultz, David. 1970. The Role of the Boyfriend in Lower Class Negro Life. In *The Family Life of Black People*, ed. C. V. Willie. Columbus, Ohio: Charles E. Merrill.

Staples, Robert. 1970. The Myth of the Black Matriarchy. *Black Scholar* 1:8–16.

Stouffer, Samuel A. 1980. *An Experimental Comparison of Statistical and Case History Methods of Attitude Research*. New York: Arno Press.

Stowe, Harriet B. 1852. *Uncle Tom's Cabin*. New York: Pocket Books.

Strauss, Anselm L. 1987. *Qualitative Analysis for Social Scientists*. New York: Cambridge University Press.

Taylor, Howard F. 1977. Playing the Dozens with Path Analysis. In *Black Separation and Social Reality*, ed. R. L. Hall. New York: Pergamon Press.

TenHouten, Warren D. 1970. The Black Family: Myth and Reality. *Psychiatry* 25: 145–173.

Traustadottir, Rannveig. 1991. Mother Who Care. *Journal of Family Issues* 12: 211–228.

U.S. Census Bureau. 2000. *Statistical Abstract of the United States*. Washington, D.C.: U.S. Government Printing Office.

———. 2001. *Statistical Abstract of the United States*. Washington, D.C.: U.S. Government Printing Office.

U.S. Department of Education. 2000. *Digest of Educational Statistics*. Washington, D.C.: U.S. Government Printing Office.

U.S. Department of Labor. 1965. *The Negro Family, A Case for National Action*. Washington, D.C.: U.S. Government Printing Office.

U.S. Office of Management and Budget. 1973. Washington, D.C.: U.S. Government Printing Office.

Valentine, Bettylou. 1978. *Hustling and Other Hard Work*. New York: Free Press.

Walker, Alice. 1982. *The Color Purple*. New York: Pocket Books.

Wallace, Walter L., ed. 1969. *Sociological Theory*. Chicago: Aldine.

Washington, Booker T. 1965. *Up From Slavery*. New York: Dell.

Wasserman, Herbert L. 1970. The Absent Father in Negro Families. In *The Family Life of Black People*, ed. C. V. Willie, 294–298. Columbus, Ohio: Merrill.

Weber, Max. 1930. *The Protestant Ethic and the Spirit of Capitalism*. London: George Allen and Unwin Ltd.

Wilkes, Paul. 1977. *Six American Families*. New York: Seabury Press.

Will, George F. 1986. Dehumanizing Blacks. *Boston Globe*, 15 February, p. 11.

Willie, Charles V. 1974. The Black Family and Social Class. *Journal of Orthopsychiatry* 44 (January): 50–60.

———. 1976. *A New Look at Black Families* 1st ed. Dix Hills, N.Y.: General Hall.

———. 1978. Black and White Middle Class Families: What They Can Teach and Learn from Each Other. *Interaction* (Winter): 12–20.

———. 1978. *The Sociology of Education*. Lexington, Mass.: Lexington Books.

———. 1981. *A New Look at Black Families* 2d ed. Dix Hills, N.Y.: General Hall.

———. 1983. *Race, Ethnicity and Socioeconomic Status*. Dix Hills, N.Y.: General Hall.

———. 1986. *Five Black Scholars*. Cambridge, Mass.: Abt Books and University Press of America.

———. 1985. *Black and White Families: A Study in Complementarity*. Dix Hills, N.Y.: General Hall.

———. 1994. *Theories of Human Social Action*. Dix Hills, N.Y.: General Hall.

Willie, Charles V., and Morton O. Wagenfeld. 1962. *Socioeconomic and Ethnic Areas*. Syracuse, N.Y.: Syracuse University Youth Development Center.

Wilson, Emily H., and Susan Mullally. 1983. *Hope and Dignity: Older Black Women of the South*. Philadelphia: Temple University Press.

Wilson, William Julius. 1978. *The Declining Significance of Race*. Chicago: University of Chicago Press.

———. 1987. *The Truly Disadvantaged*. Chicago: University of Chicago Press.

Wrobel, Paul. 1976. Polish American Men: As Workers, as Husbands, and as Fathers. Paper presented at American Association for the Advancement of Science, 18–24 February, Boston, Mass.

Index

About the Authors

Charles Vert Willie is Professor Emeritus, Harvard University Graduate School of Education, and is the author of twenty-five books on issues of race, education, and urban communities. His areas of research include desegregation, higher education, public health, race relations, urban community problems, and family life. He has served as vice president of the American Sociological Association and president of the Eastern Sociological Society. Willie is the author of more than one hundred articles and twenty-five books on issues of race, education, urban communities, and the family. A graduate of Morehouse College and Atlanta University, Willie received a doctoral degree in sociology from the Maxwell School of Syracuse University. He was presented with the Distinguished Family Scholar Award by the Society for the Study of Social Problems in 1986 and the DuBois-Johnson-Frazier Award from the American Sociological Association in 1994. He and his wife, Mary Sue Conklin Willie, live in Concord, Massachusetts. They have three children: Sarah Susannah Willie, Martin Charles Willie, and James Theodore Willie.

Richard Reddick is a doctoral candidate in administration, planning, and social policy at the Harvard Graduate School of Education, and he serves as a member of the Harvard Educational Review Editorial Board. Reddick has worked as a research assistant on the National Campus Diversity Project at Harvard with Dr. Dean Whitla. His professional experiences include teaching at the historic E. O. Smith Education Center in Houston, Texas, with Teach For America from 1995 to 1997; working in student affairs at the Massachusetts Institute of Technology, Cal Poly-San Luis Obispo, and Emory University; and serving as a School Director with Teach For America in Houston. Reddick completed a master's degree at Harvard in 1998 and is a 1995 Distinguished Graduate of the University of Texas at Austin. He and his wife Sherry live in Watertown, Massachusetts.